MW01531859

LITTLE ME,
I WILL LIVE NOW

A JOURNEY FROM IDENTITY CRISIS
TO WAKING THE DREAMER

ISIAH D. TATUM

AUTHOR elite
ACADEMY

Little Me, I Will Live Now © 2019 by Isiah D. Tatum.
All rights reserved.
Printed in the United States of America
Published by Author Academy Elite
PO Box 43, Powell, OH 43035
www.AuthorAcademyElite.com

All rights reserved. This book contains material protected under International and Federal Copyright Laws and Treaties. Any unauthorized reprint or use of this material is prohibited. No part of this book may be reproduced or transmitted in any form or by any means, electronic or mechanical, including photocopying, recording, or by any information storage and retrieval system, without express written permission from the author.

Identifiers:
LCCN: 2019907000
ISBN: 978-1-64085-719-3 (paperback)
ISBN: 978-1-64085-720-9 (hardback)
ISBN: 978-1-64085-721-6 (eBook)

Available in paperback, hardback, and e-book
All Scripture quotations, unless otherwise indicated, are taken from the Holy Bible, New International Version®, NIV®. Copyright © 1973, 1978, 1984 by Biblica, Inc.TM Used by permission of Zondervan. All rights reserved worldwide.

Other Scripture references are from the following sources:
The Message (MSG), copyright © 1993, 2002, 2018 by Eugene H. Peterson. Used by permission of NavPress. All rights reserved. Represented by Tyndale House Publishers, Inc.

Any Internet addresses (websites, blogs, etc.) and telephone numbers printed in this book are offered as a resource. They are not intended in any way to be or imply an endorsement by Author Academy Elite, nor does Author Academy Elite vouch for the content of these sites and numbers for the life of this book.

I dedicate this book to every dreamer. You were created for this very moment. Do not shrink back or hide your gifts any longer because the world needs you. Believe in yourself and dream again!

CONTENTS

PREFACE

I am writing this book because I have been thinking about you. I've even had dreams about some of you. As you begin to read this book, whether by recommendation or due to general interest, I know you are one of the ones I have dreamed about who will one day positively change the world. Yes, you! You are the next—Grammy Award-winning songwriter, Academy Award-winning actress, mother, father, multi-million-dollar business owner, Nobel Peace Prize recipient, the New York Times best-selling author—the list goes on endlessly.

However, I have also been praying for you because I am aware of the opposition you face. Through experience, I know how it has been holding you hostage and prevented you from achieving your dreams. In short, this opposition holds the key that unlock your destiny. What's this opposition? It's the Little You.

I know this seems confusing now, but it will all make sense as we start on this journey. Have you felt defeated because of past failures due to fear? Do the words of someone from your childhood cripple you from believing in yourself? Have you given up the pursuit of your dreams because of mistakes that you made as a young adult? If you've answered yes to these questions, you are reading the right book.

Let me offer a warning. This journey will bring you into contact with your truth: the emotions, pain, and memories that have invaded your thoughts for years. Please do not get discouraged. Confronting your pain is necessary to get over the barrier that stands between you and purpose. You should be excited because you will finally be able to start the process of moving on with your life and become the great person you were created to be. It will all be worth it in the end!

I emphasize *truth* because I had to walk through this process, and to this day, I am still healing. You will see that throughout this book, as I open up my intimate pain, struggles, and insecurities to help you because I was once held hostage by the Little Me.

The world needs our testimonies and dreams to come to fruition because it gives people who have lost hope to know they can overcome and win. I can't wait to hear the stories you will share after you have read this book. You are great! You are a world-changer! Never lose sight of this.

Let's get this journey started. By the end of this, you will finally be alive! Now say to yourself, "Little Me, I will live now!"

1

THAT DAY

"Derwin, come downstairs and eat your cereal, honey!"

Pulling the covers over his head with a little grunt, Derwin says, "Yes, ma'am, I will be right down."

A petite, beautiful woman with brown eyes and perfect skin frantically looks for her cell phone, pours cereal, slams the cabinet doors, and shouts,

"I can't believe she's late again. I'm going to be late for work, and Mr. Thomas is not having it."

She picks up her cell phone, "Sarah, this is Karen. Please pick up your phone and give me a call back. I can't be late anymore, or I'll get fired. You know where to reach me."

She slams the phone on the counter with so much frustration a small tear slips from the corner of her right eye.

Derwin, wearing his favorite red dinosaur pajamas, comes downstairs with caution as if a madwoman was in the kitchen.

"Is everything okay, Mom?"

"Yes, son, everything is okay. Sarah is late again, and I have no one to watch you. Here's your breakfast."

"Don't worry about it, Mom, I am a man now."

Laughing, she walks up to him and grabs his cheeks, "There's no way I'm leaving my 10-year-old "man" by himself."

Derwin sticks his chest out and responds with a deep voice, "Yes, you can, Karen."

"Boy, you better not call me by my first name!"

Kissing him on the forehead and patting the kiss, she says, "Nope, I'm not doing it!"

Stopping in her tracks, Karen recalls a conversation she had with Ms. Sullivan down the hallway.

"Ms. Sullivan's grandchildren are visiting her for the summer. She said if I ever needed anything to ask."

Derwin screams out, "No!"

"What?" his mom asks.

"I can't go over to Ms. Sullivan's house."

"Why not?"

"Because she smells like a hundred cigarettes! And I can't get second-hand smoke. Don't you know that causes cancer? I have asthma."

"You are something else little boy. And you don't have asthma!"

They both laugh hysterically, and she runs down five flights of stairs to knock on Ms. Sullivan's door.

"Ms. Sullivan, it's Karen. Please answer the door."

Answering the door with haste, a heavy-set African American lady with a floral robe and one roller hanging from her bang answers the door and blows smoke in Karen's face.

"How may I help you, honey? Is everything okay?"

Coughing from the smoke inhalation, "Yes, ma'am, everything is okay. Well, not really."

Speeding up her speech like an auctioneer, she continues. "Derwin's babysitter is a no call, no show, again, and I have no one to watch him. I can't be late or miss any more days, or my boss is going to fire me. I don't know what to do. You had mentioned if I ever needed you to watch him, you would."

Ms. Sullivan perks up and says, "I told you about those millennials. They can't be trusted. Yes, bring that cute little boy on down here. My niece and nephews are here for the summer. He'll have fun with us."

Before Karen could say thank you, her phone rang. It was Sarah.

"Sarah, I've been calling you all morning. What's going on?"

"Ms. Karen, I'm sorry, but I will no longer be able to keep Derwin. I've found another job that pays more, and with me being in school, I need all the money I can get. I am so sorry! Talk to you later."

As the voice on the other end disappears, Karen looks dumbfounded at the phone and tears begin to run down her face. She slowly slides down the wall.

"What's wrong, baby?" Ms. Sullivan asks.

"What am I going to do? My babysitter just quit on me, and I have no one to watch Derwin for the summer. It is so hard being a single parent."

"Say no more," declares Ms. Sullivan. "I will watch him for the summer. No charge to you. It will be my pleasure."

Karen jumps up and hugs Ms. Sullivan with all her might.

"Thank you so, so much! You have no idea what a lifesaver you are right now! I will repay you!"

She runs back upstairs to get Derwin.

"You be good and respectful, you hear?"

"Yes, ma'am."

"Ms. Sullivan is going to look after you for the summer while I'm at work. Play well with her grandkids. Okay?"

"Yes, Mama."

"Give me a kiss. Mama loves you."

They embrace, and she sprints towards the elevator.

Ms. Sullivan motions to Derwin. "Come on in, baby. You're in great hands now. Let me introduce you to my grandbabies."

"Over there," she points to the boy by the window, "that's my thirteen-year-old grandson, C.J."

C.J. looks up briefly from the Xbox game, "What's up?" Immediately he goes back to complete focus after his opponent tackles him on Madden.

"Over there, you have Ryan. He's ten just like you."

Ryan is a ball of energy and immediately greets Derwin with a question. "Would you like to play Legos with me? His imagination is out of this world.

"We can build a castle with a big fortress from the Galanytes—the nemeses to the Univites."

"That sounds awesome," Derwin responds with excitement.

Before Ms. Sullivan can say another word, there is a loud bang in the kitchen.

"C.J., where is your little sister Amy?"

"I don't know, Grandma. She was in the kitchen the last time I saw her."

With a grin on her face and covered in flour, the little four-year-old makes her entrance.

"Oh no, little girl. Let's get you cleaned up."

"Derwin, the bathroom is down that hallway." Ms. Sullivan points to the dark hall. "My brother Randy is in that room next to the bathroom. He only comes out to eat and use the bathroom."

After being acclimated to the new babysitting digs, Derwin and Ryan become best buds and play all day.

Ms. Sullivan made a great lunch along with some good, sweet lemonade. After about four glasses, Derwin needs to use the bathroom badly.

"Ms. Sullivan, where's the bathroom again?"

"Down that hall to the left, baby." She motions toward the door.

Derwin looks down the dark and distant hallway.

He begins to walk down the hallway with caution. He gets to the end of the hall but instead of going left, the open door and loud TV noise draw him in.

Peeking around the corner, Derwin sees a dark, musky room with one light on in the closet, clothes on the floor, an unmade bed with the mattress hanging over the edge, a La-Z-Boy chair, and an old TV with an antenna displaying the daily news.

A deep voice startles him. He hadn't noticed anyone in the room.

"What are you doing little boy?"

When he turns around, he sees a muscular, 6'4, bald man wearing a white tank top and shorts.

"Uhm. Nothing, sir. Looking for the bathroom."

"What's your name, little man?" the giant asks with a terrifying stare. Derwin bites his bottom lip to keep from crying out.

Just a little bit terrified, Derwin answers, "My name is . . . my name is . . . Der . . . win."

"Don't be afraid, little man, I won't hurt you. My name is Randy, and the bathroom is that way."

"Thank you," Derwin answers sheepishly.

He walks down what seems to be a one-mile hallway and goes into the bathroom. He turns around to close the door and finds Randy looking at him before fully closing the door.

There's a knock at the door, and Derwin jumps. It's Ms. Sullivan.

"Derwin, is everything okay in there? Your mom is here to pick you up."

He runs out of the bathroom and jumps into his mom's arms, and plants a big kiss on her cheek.

"Whoa, son! I'm glad to see you, too! Thanks, Ms. Sullivan. I really appreciate it."

"You're welcome, baby."

Karen looks at Derwin, "Say thank you to Ms. Sullivan."

"Thank you, Ms. Sullivan. See you tomorrow, Ryan!"

"See you later, Derwin!" Ryan responds with a wave and excitement.

Karen and Derwin walk up the five flights of steps slowly.

"How was your day today, baby?"

"My day was *great*! Ryan is my best friend. C.J. played video games all day, and little Amy is a monster."

"A monster?" his mom asks.

"Yes, she gets into everything. We had to chase her around the house all day until she took a nap. Did I mention Ms. Sullivan can really cook? I love to eat! And," Derwin pauses, "her brother, Randy, never leaves his room."

"Randy?" she interrupts him. "Who is Randy?"

"That's Ms. Sullivan's brother."

Perplexed and confused, she responds, "I never knew she had a brother that lived with her. Okay, glad you had a great time over there. You'll be going back tomorrow."

"As long as Ryan is there, it's going to be a lot of fun."

The next day, Derwin beats his mom out of bed. He is dressed and ready to go to Ms. Sullivan's house before Karen is dressed to go.

"Mom, is it time to go yet? I'm ready to go hang with my friend, Ryan."

Patting her hair with squinted eyes, his mom says, "Derwin, give me a moment to get dressed, and I will take you there in an hour."

Derwin is already sitting by the door with his favorite red dinosaur backpack filled with toys for him and Ryan.

When it is time to go, Derwin rushes out the door and runs down the hallway. Trying her best to lock the door, Karen yells, "Derwin, wait up. Don't go down those stairs without me."

He insists on getting down there as quickly as possible. Derwin runs to the door and knocks frantically.

Ms. Sullivan asks, "Who is it?" with a forceful tone.

"It's Derwin."

She opens the door and blows cigarette smoke in his face. Derwin starts to cough and fan the smoke from his nostrils. "Ah, Ms. Sullivan, enough with the secondhand smoke."

Karen is running trying to catch up in the distance.

"I'm so sorry, Ms. Sullivan. Derwin is really excited and apparently couldn't get down here fast enough."

"It's okay, baby. Come on in, son. I'll see you later on today, Karen."

"Give me a hug and a kiss, son."

Derwin embraces his mother and follows up with, "I love you, Mom!"

The door shuts behind him.

Derwin runs over to Ryan, excited because he wants to know what adventure they'll have today. He brought some awesome toys from his home collection.

But Ryan wasn't his typical, upbeat self. He had a dazed look on his face.

"Oh, hey, Derwin, buddy."

"What's wrong?" Derwin asks in a concerned voice. "Are you ready to . . . ?"

Before he could complete his sentence, Ryan interrupts him, "Nothing. Nothing is wrong."

In the background, the boys can hear Ms. Sullivan saying, "Oh no, I've run out of cigarettes, milk, and diapers for the baby. I need to go to the store. C.J., grab Amy, and you ride with me to the store. You know I can't keep up with that little girl. Ryan and Derwin, you stay here with Uncle Randy."

Ryan, like a sprinter, runs to Ms. Sullivan, "Grandma, may I please go with you?"

"I'll be right back, baby. It won't take us long. Just stay here."

Tears come to Ryan's eyes, but they don't faze Ms. Sullivan.

Ms. Sullivan yells as she walks out the door, "Randy, we'll be right back. You'll need to keep an eye on the boys."

There is no response. The door closes, and Ryan jumps at the loud thump.

Ryan immediately grabs Derwin's hand and instructs him. "Derwin, today's game is hide and seek. The person who hides the best wins."

Derwin is up for the challenge. Randy's door creeps open, and Ryan is already hidden.

"Ryan, where did you go?" Derwin whispers. There is no answer.

Derwin could hear footsteps getting closer and closer. So, he runs to find a hiding spot.

A couple of seconds later, Randy's deep voice rings through the house, "Where are you, little boys? Uncle Randy is here and knows you all are playing hide and seek. The one I catch is it and has to come with me."

He searches around the apartment. He sees Derwin's red dinosaur backpack outside the cabinet where he is hiding.

The cabinet door opens swiftly, and Randy shouts, "Boo! I found you!"

Derwin jumps back in the cabinet and hits his head.

"You have to come with me."

"Where are we going?" Derwin asks.

"You'll see in a minute. I have some goodies in my room. Do you like candy?"

"Yes, I love candy!"

"Well, follow me. You're the winner of today's game."

"I thought if you get caught, you're the loser."

"That's not how I play. The person caught wins a prize."

As they walk down the hallway, Derwin sees where Ryan is hiding, but Derwin doesn't say anything. What Derwin sees puzzles him. Ryan waves with a sad face and immediately closes his eyes and puts his hands over his ears.

Derwin becomes uneasy and immediately looks down that dark hallway.

As they get closer to the room, Randy, with a welcoming smile on his face, directs Derwin to go in the room. It is dark, and the only light comes from the closet and the old TV showing the daily news.

As Derwin approaches the doorway cautiously, Randy instructs, "Come on in, and shut that door behind you."

2

THE WOUND

In the previous chapter, you met a little boy by the name of Derwin, but you never got a chance to know how his story ended. I will tell you. Derwin's innocence was stolen from him that day. How do I know? (Well, I did write the story, but that's not the point.) I know because Derwin's story is similar to mine.

The word "innocence" is often associated with babies and children because they are harmless individuals who seem to have no ill intent. *Aw, they are so cute. I want to squeeze those little cheeks.* They easily trust and have the greatest imaginations. Children, as far as they know, can do anything they imagine. Webster's Dictionary even defines innocence as the lack of experience with the world and the bad things that happen in life.[1]

Growing up, one of my favorite cartoons was Rugrats. Every Saturday, it was a routine to get a big bowl of Cap n' Crunch, turn to channel 27, and indulge in the diaper baby brigade. Tommy, Chucky, Phil & Lil, Angelica, Susie, Kimmie, Dil, and Spike always seemed to amaze me with their imaginations. During each show, they took viewers on an adventure to the most magical places their minds could conjure. They exuded courage, faced many fears, worked together, conquered, and came back to reality. The most intriguing part about this show was that these babies had their parents fooled. I screamed at the television, "Can't you hear these babies talking?" Unbeknownst to the parents, these kids were real-life heroes, but instead, the parents saw them as their babies. How could they know? These babies had mastered the art of a "double life." When the parents weren't around, the babies saved the world and fixed people's problems. When the parents were around, the kids acted like babies because the parents would never think these babies were able to speak. After watching cartoons, it was time to go outside and create adventures of my own.

My family owned a large field on the side of my uncle's house where kids in the neighborhood frequently played softball. There were kids of all ages from ten to teenagers, and we would play until it was too dark to see anymore, we got called to help out at our family grocery store, or it was time to go home. Those games were almost every day during the summer because there wasn't much to do in the rural area I called home. My cousins' friends, who stayed with their grandma during the summer or lived in the neighborhood, would come down to play and hang out with us. After a game of softball, we always had to clean up the field, or we would feel the wrath of my uncle. One day, my cousins got called into the house, so I was stuck with one of my cousin's older friends cleaning up the field. He said he had to use the bathroom, so being that it was the country, we were taught to go on the side of the house. I was the only one left, so when the guy screamed, "Isiah, come here and look at this snake," I ran. Being eight and naive, I had never seen a snake before, so I was curious, but it wasn't the type of snake I expected. When it was all over, I ran home with a new life secret: I had been molested. That was the start of me being a professional mask wearer and liar. Every summer he would come, the same thing would happen over and over again. It was like I had "Touch Me" on my forehead because it would happen with other teen guys at school, church, and sleepovers. I could not shake this frequent occurrence, and it messed up my life from that moment.

Being molested was a memory that haunted me for years. The little boy in me was crushed, and my identity was stolen. Instead of playing with Power Rangers and trucks, I was forced to keep a "secret" that would make me a loner and an actor of sorts. Not only did it affect me mentally, physically, emotionally, and spiritually, it also tried to steal my dreams and my future.

For years, I could never process why it was happening to me, and I had a plethora of questions. How could this happen to me? Who am I? Was it my fault? Can I tell anyone, and if I do, will they believe me? Can anyone see me dying on the inside? Ultimately, the unanswered questions brought a lot of baggage into my life because it was overwhelming. Not only did I have to deal with internal struggles and emotions, but I also had to deal with the external—people.

In middle school, everyone's hormones were raging. Relationships and sex were the goals—this was the norm. However, this was not the norm for me because I was fighting to understand who I was as a person, more importantly, as a young man. As I started meeting new people, I found out quickly that I was no longer in elementary school. People weren't as polite, they didn't want to be your friend, and recess was a thing of the past. In middle school, you were faced with the *"truth!"* I was a chubby sixth-grader raised in the country who had a secret of being molested.

Often when I walked down the hallway, there were groups of people staring, pointing, and laughing at me. Being molested by males at a young age brought about sexual confusion, which created an inner struggle with identity. I would hear, spoken in undertones, "There goes that fat faggot, Isiah." "Yes, that's the guy they said is gay." The whispering would go on for days, weeks, months, and years. What made it even worse was that I heard teachers talking about me as well. It was too much to take! I felt all alone, so I shut down. It was so bad that I would hide in the mornings, purposefully miss the bus, and skip school to avoid the words of people. No one hit me physically, but the blows of their words destroyed this already unidentified boy. I was *humiliated*!

After a while, I built this world that protected me from ever being hurt again, which also made me a victim, and I wouldn't allow people to love me. I became angry, depressed, shy, timid, unsure, rejected, addicted to pornography, jealous, and envious because my life didn't look like the "normal" person's life. I was deeply wounded and shamed!

To deal with this pain and not be teased, I had to create this "perfect boy" image. The invented person was my escape from reality. We have all seen or know this person: he's very successful, everyone likes him, and he can do nothing wrong, and he's perfect—at least in the sight of people. In school, I was the most popular kid, class and school president, and successful, had it all together, and I was destined for greatness. I wanted to be this person so bad because I was struggling with low self-esteem and sought praise and validation from people, which was a crippling drug. I got high off of people's compliments but still had to go home to reality and internal emptiness. This pattern would go on for years—even into adulthood.

I had to learn the truth that I was never created to carry the burden of perfectionism. In the long run, it just does not work. My character flaws started to show. The pretender I portrayed to the outside world conflicted with who I truly was on the inside. I chose to self-medicate the pain with perfection and success. These wounds hindered me from achieving real progress in the areas of my life that I desired to succeed in. From a young age, I knew I wanted to travel the world as a singer. I was a big dreamer! However, after being made fun of and laughed at, I tucked that dream away and stopped believing it would come true. I was disappointed in myself. So, I became successful in business, which was not a bad thing, but it was at the cost of not living my dream.

I became fed up with living a mediocre life. The years started to fly by, and I was nowhere near my dream or purpose. That worried me because there was a possibility I would be eighty years old and reflect on my life with eyes of regret—all because of a wounded little boy.

Did I have the right to stay a victim and be mad at the world? *Absolutely*! However, after playing the victim for so many years, it became tiring. I lost hope. Deep down on the inside, something was telling me there was more to life. My dreams were calling me. First, I needed healing before moving forward. I needed to know my true identity.

Like me, I'm sure you have memories and scars in your life that have kept you from getting back up and starting again. You feel the pain is just too unbearable, and it is more comfortable to sit back and survive life versus facing the risk of getting wounded again.

Do you want to know a secret? You may also identify with little Derwin. You may have questions you've asked since you were harmed somehow. Your initial response is probably, "I've never been sexually abused." You may be right, but you do have that one day that changed your life forever. It is ingrained into your memory, and the feelings and emotions are still there as if that day happened yesterday. It may be verbal and physical abuse, abandonment by your parents, being bullied in school, someone saying you weren't good enough, or your spouse leaving you for someone else—the list is almost infinite.

Stop for a moment, be still, and ask yourself—*what incident(s) changed the course of my life? Where have I been wounded? What is affecting my everyday life?* Now it is all starting to come back. For so long, these memories have been buried so deep inside your subconscious mind that you've forgotten about the incidents and ultimately made them a part of who you are. You were wounded.

My reason for writing this book and sharing my story is to show you that we must birth our dreams and ideas. Before that can happen, however, we have to know and understand what's hindering us, and it's typically wounds that have been untreated and self-defeating beliefs about ourselves. This book is not one of those counseling books where I tell you thirty ways to be healed and free, because that is beyond my education and expertise. I highly recommend you see a professional counselor who has been certified and trained to deal with trauma and can provide you with the guidance to navigate through the pain. Now this book does show you how to confront the Little You, how to prevent your past from derailing who you were created to be, and how to use it as a change-agent in the world. You have greatness in you. It's time to let it out!

3

LETTER FROM BIG YOU

Dear Little Me,

It is great to finally get this letter to you, as I have a lot to share with you while there is still time. You will never believe what has been going on in here for all these years. When you were little, you consistently imagined the unthinkable and dreamed of changing the world. Your heart beat rapidly, and your mind raced with excitement at the thought of you becoming everything you dreamt. It was cool to see you act out different imaginations because you believed in those things. You proclaimed your wishes, hopes, and accomplishments loudly, and it did my heart good to see you were on the path to becoming a great individual—*me*. I was sure the whole world would know your name because they would see the ideas, inventions, and other talents you possessed. We were sure to make it with this type of thriving environment.

Then the unthinkable happened—*life*. I remember hearing you cry in the darkness of your room when some harsh words were spoken to you. These words slapped you across the face and wounded you deeply. I began to feel this pain that knocked the breath out of me. Lies bombarded your thoughts that you were not good enough, too fat, unworthy, ugly, and poor. I began to scream. *Don't believe them! You're the opposite of what they're saying!* But you didn't hear me. As these things were happening, I began to see tall, cemented walls being built by the pain and ugly emotions. Before I knew it, each circumstance put me in chains and behind bars. The walls kept getting closer and closer and closer.

Help Me! Help us! I'm suffocating here, and I'm claustrophobic. The only way to free us is by believing in yourself again. I promise you won't regret what you'll become because of it. Feed me with your positive thoughts because I'm starving. Dream and believe again because it reminds me that I will one day be free. Trust again! Listen to me, you were never meant to stay in these conditions, and I'm tormented by thoughts of not becoming who we were created to be. It's a prison inside here, and only you can help me. *Help! Help! Help! Help!*

With Urgency,
The Big You

Wake up calls are life's way of telling us the preciousness and value of time. Take Big You from the letter at the beginning of the chapter. Big You wants to get the warning to you that if you don't believe and dream again, you won't fulfill your life's real purpose. Time is one thing in life that we do not get back. We can always make more money, take more trips, get more jobs, but we can never get more time. Wake up calls are also the very thing that makes us realize we aren't here forever, and we need to figure out why we were placed here on this earth. A great man named Dr. Myles Munroe said, "The richest place on earth is the graveyard." Most people asked him why he thought so. He replied, "Because, many people's dreams die with them. Books, businesses, inventions, recipes, and cures all go into the grave with the person to never positively affect the world." *Wow*!

My most significant wake-up call came the summer before my senior year in high school. I remember when Facebook notes were the trend. Everybody was posting a poem, a love story, or something about his or her life. There was an influx of self-made philosophers, authors, preachers, and people who had life "all figured out." Well, let me be honest. I thought I was one of those people too. I felt like Tyler Perry reading the message boards after he'd release a new movie or play. Facebook notes allow you to see people's comments on how they related to your note and how their lives might be changed. Who would have thought that one thing I wrote in 2007 would change my life forever?

A LITTLE SOMETHING FROM THE HEART

July 11, 2007, at 2:09 a.m.

Well, I usually don't do this note stuff, but I really need to get this off my chest. I never thought I would go through so much all at one time as I have this summer. My stepdad passed away, and I didn't know what to do, so all I did was cry. I'm not the crying type, but I guess I fooled myself. A true angel from the Lord came into my life in the nick of time to walk my family through something for which we weren't prepared. I am on a journey called "right now," and some of you don't know what life is and how valuable it is.

I think it's time for people to start being truthful with themselves and stop beating around the bush! Everyone knows me as being the "Big Man" on campus (literally) or the boy that sings gospel all the time. Well, the truth is I was being something that I wasn't, and I said to myself, *The way you're living is not worth you singing gospel trying to deliver people.* Basically, I had a reality check, and I was someone I'm not. I would try to fit in with people that I couldn't piece myself with. I always wanted attention—and I would always get it. What all this boils down to is that my whole life was a lie. I would smile in your face and then talk about you when you walked away, gossip about you. I had a chance to hear comments about me from people that shocked and hurt me. I got past it because I don't listen to what people say, but come on, people—I care! Also, I had a chance to feel alone.

Hats off to the people who don't have friends because it's not a good feeling—no one to talk to or to hang around with, and I was like, not Isiah Tatum. Yes, me! But you know what, I'm grateful for that feeling because I had a chance to get to know God and get to know the real Isiah D'shun Tatum (don't steal my identity, you thieves), who is a great young man about to burst onto the scene.

"Isiah, why don't you have a girlfriend?" is the number one question people ask me, which is understandable, but let's set the record straight. To be someone or bring someone into your life, you have to make sure your life is whole, because it will be hell if you try to bring someone into something that is not stable. Why do you think so many relationships fail? My special someone is always going to be there because God placed her on this earth to be only with me. I just have to find her.

"Seek and you shall find, knock and the door will be opened" (Matthew 7:7). God has weeded some people out of my life because they are hindering me from getting to where I'm going. If you don't like me, I still love you, but you are a hindrance, then I'll say see you later. It doesn't stop there. There are going to be more people taken out of my life, and God is going to show me the rest. So if you are one of those people, bad luck. All I'm asking is if everyone would forget everything about gossip and the lies about me and would recognize there is a new me, I would greatly appreciate it. And people, learn from me—stop living a fake life! It's noticeable, and it doesn't look right. Live your life, but make sure it is a pleasing one!

One Love,
Tatum

Later on, I would find out that at the moment and time I was writing my note, my life was changing forever. Early in the morning on Wednesday, July 11, 2007, I woke up and felt the need to cook a big breakfast for the whole family. We were from the country, so it was going to be one of those Klumps' feasts with bacon, sausage, eggs, pancakes, oatmeal, biscuits, fruit, and whatever else we could throw in there. I went around the house to determine what everyone wanted to eat. My sister and friend were up for the feast. My brother walked in the door and said he was hungry. The last person who I needed to ask was my dad. The time was about 9 or 10 a.m., so it was unusual for my dad to be home. He was the worker who left the house at 7 a.m. and didn't come back until midnight. All the kids were under the assumption he was tired.

I walked into his room—because we didn't believe in knocking—and asked, "Daddy, do you want some breakfast?" There was no answer. I figured he probably hadn't heard me because he had to sleep with a CPAP machine to help with his sleep apnea. I walked closer to ask, "Daddy, would you like some bacon or sausage?" No answer. As I got closer to him, I said, "Daddy, Daddy. Do you want some breakfast?" He continued to sleep, but an irritating noise began to ring in my left ear. I turned to the left, and the machine screamed "*Alert!*" My stomach dropped to the floor. I started to panic and started calling his name, "Daddy. Daddy. *Daddy! Daddy!*" His arm was not under the covers, so I lifted it to the ceiling while calling his name, and it fell with such force.

I pulled the covers back, and I was faced with the truth that my dad was dead because he had urinated in his underwear. I yelled, "Call 9-1-1. Dial 9-1-1!" Hearing my panic, my brother ran in and started calling our dad's name. My sister jumped onto the bed while she was on the phone with 9-1-1, and she felt him and yelled, "He's *cold!*" By this time, I had blanked out, was numb, and hearing voices that said, *You're going to lose your mind.* Before I knew it, my uncles and aunt were in the room, moving my Dad's body from his bed to the floor so my aunt could do CPR. After many failed attempts, the anguished cry from my aunt confirmed he was gone forever. Who would have ever thought I would find my dad dead in our home the same day and about the same time I had written that Facebook note?

Can I be honest? That was the *worst* day but also the *best* day of my life. Let me explain: before this event, my life was headed down a destructive path. I was a public success but a private failure, as mentioned in the Facebook note. Everything about my life was based on materialistic and superficial things: cars, houses, clothes, phones, money, and popularity. You name it; I had it. We were in the process of moving into a five thousand square foot house, and my dad said he would buy me the new 2008 Escalade EXT for graduation. So, life was good, well, at least I thought it was good. I will admit, I was a spoiled brat. I was a selfish individual who only cared about 'self.' That was not good at all, because the life I knew all crumbled in a matter of hours. The home, money, and cars were all taken away. My sister and I were forced to live a lifestyle worlds apart from what we were used to living.

We all go through seasons of questioning why certain things had to happen. My dad's passing occurred the summer before my senior year of high school, right when I needed my dad most. I needed him to walk me through my senior year when adversities came. I needed him to pay for my cap and gown. I needed him to be there to cheer for me as I walked across the stage. I needed him to say I love you and am proud of you. I just needed him there. It wasn't until college that I got the answer to my question: "God, why did you take my dad away from me?" The response I received went like this. "Personal choices and consequences was the ultimate reason he left so soon—not because I took him away. In your case, he was your god."

This statement hit me like a ton of bricks because He started showing me how my dad was my god. "You wanted him to supply everything for you. You looked to him when you needed comfort and direction. That's my job! No one else knows and loves you as I do. You were going to delay your destiny if your dad hadn't passed away."

Ever since that conversation with God, I've gained peace about my father's passing. It really shocked me because when I wrote the Facebook note, it was just after my dad had passed in his sleep. His death confirmed the lines I wrote in the note: "God has weeded some people out of my life because they are hindering me from getting to where I'm going. It doesn't stop there, it is going to be more people, and God is going to show me the rest." Wow! To be truthful, I wouldn't be the person I am today if my father was still living, but I do miss him.

I'll never forget the day my dad died because that was the day the world lost a great dreamer who accomplished what he set out to do. My dad had quit his post office job after 21 years and started a house building company. Sweet Dreams Homebuilders became the number two house building company in Arkansas. Not only was he an accomplished builder, but he was a serial entrepreneur with several successful companies. One of the most significant aspects of his dream of being a business owner was that he could supply jobs to those that society abandoned. He was a loving and caring person who believed in giving people a second chance. Everyone wanted to be around him. Two years after my dad's passing, one of the workers came up to me and said, "I can't thank your father enough for believing in me. He gave me a second chance at life to feed and provide for my family." That's when I had learned the purpose of our dreams were to give people hope and for building a legacy to help individuals have a second chance at life. From that moment forward, it was my mission to become everything God created me to be. I didn't want to be one of the ones Dr. Myles Munroe talked about allowing their dreams to die with them. That doesn't do any good. I knew it was time to start living my life so that I would die with nothing else to give.

Today is your wakeup call. Your future self is calling you now while begging and pleading for you to wake up and become who you were created to be. If you sat face to face with your future self today, what would that self say to you? What possibilities could you be missing out on by staying where you are today? You owe it not only to yourself but also to those whose lives are connected to yours. I pray and hope it doesn't take someone you love passing away for you to know that time is precious and you have limited time here on this Earth. However, your legacy can and will live on for generations if you decide today that you are going to move forward into greatness. What will you choose?

4

HOW MUCH LONGER?

Don't' let your fear, ego, feelings of unworthiness, and entitlement keep you frozen. Wasted opportunity can lead to feeling like you've wasted your life because you didn't achieve your dreams. Take Roger, for example—a seventy-year-old man who called into the 700 Club because he never reached his goals.

"Thanks for watching the 700 Club today. I'm Pat Robertson and be sure to call 1-800-971-2555 for one of our prayer partners to pray with you about your dreams and visions today. Until next time."

Workers drop everything they are doing, scurry to their respective cubicles, and a sea of voices clash as phones ring simultaneously.

"Thanks for calling the 700 Club, this is David. How may I help you today?"

A timid and raspy voice rises from the silence, "Hello, David. My name is Roger, and I just watched Pat talk about dreams and visions on today's 700 Club."

"Yes, sir, you're correct. Is there anything I can pray with you about concerning your dreams and visions?"

A long pause ensues as the caller seems to wrestles with the decision.

"Uh…yes, please. But before you do, I'd like to tell you a little bit about my ideas."

"I'd love to hear about your ideas. Could you do me a favor and speak up a little bit. It is hard to hear you."

"So sorry about that. I will try my best. I get nervous when speaking to people."

"That's no problem at all, sir. Please share your idea."

"Yes, I would like to start a fishing pole line for fishermen in my town. I'd also like to start a t-shirt company with the many designs I have had in my head for years."

"These sound like amazing ideas, and I'd love to pray with you about them. Let me ask you this question: What's keeping you from moving forward with these ideas?"

Another long pause hovered over the conversation, but this time, Roger began to hyperventilate and cry hysterically.

"I can't seem to move forward with the ideas I have because of my father. When I was young, my father was very angry and abusive to us. One day, he bought me a fishing pole and had asked if I would like to go fishing with him. I was thrilled that it would be just the two of us. That was one of the best feelings in the world. We were having a great time at the lake. Suddenly, a fish caught on to my hook, and I wasn't ready for it. Before I knew it, my fishing pole went into the water. I'll never forget the look of disgust on his face. My dad became furious and beat me until my nose started to bleed. He called me stupid, good for nothing, a failure. I can never live down the words he spoke to me. They play over and over in my head. My father died thirty years ago, and it still affects me."

"Roger, take a moment to breathe and calm down for a brief moment. I am so sorry this happened to you."

"Thanks. It is hurtful, and I feel like a failure because I am seventy years old and can't move forward with these ideas.

I just wanted to make my father proud, but I see that's not going to happen. You know what, have a great day."

"Wait, Roger! I still have to..."

The call ends.

Let that sink in for a moment. This man, at the time, was seventy years old, and his father passed away thirty years prior. The incident he recalled with his father happened when he was just ten years old. That's sixty years of being locked in a mental prison, and to be quite honest, a wasted life and potential. Can you imagine who this man could have been? He could have been the next president, teacher, or surgeon. Who knows? He could have become just a simple father who loved his wife and kids, but these things were taken away from him.

Life is going to deal us blows, and sometimes those blows come from the individuals who are supposed to take care of and love us unconditionally. It hurts! In Roger's case, it stole his entire life. This story is very vivid to me, and I had to share it because some lessons must be learned from Roger's story.

a. We have to identify the source, incident, or pain that is hindering us. Once we determine that, we have to take the proper next steps to get help. If not, it will impact our entire lives.

b. We cannot live our lives and dreams for people's approval. If so, we will never move forward with our sincere hearts' desires. Ultimately, the price is an unfulfilled life.

Experiencing trauma of any kind is hard, especially during childhood. The mind is still developing and gaining its patterns and ways of processing things. When someone has experienced trauma, nobody can take away the fact the

26

individual was a victim. He or she needs time and specialized counseling to process through the pain, trauma, and hurt. It is a process. However, if not careful, that individual can take on the "victim mentality." Here is a story from the Bible (John 5:1-9) of a man who had this mindset:

Sometime later, Jesus went up to Jerusalem for one of the Jewish festivals. In Jerusalem, near the Sheep Gate, there is a pool, which in Aramaic is called Bethesda and which is surrounded by five covered colonnades. Here a great number of disabled people used to lay—the blind, the lame, the paralyzed. One who was there had been an invalid for thirty-eight years. When Jesus saw him lying there and learned that he had been in this condition for a long time, he asked him, "Do you want to get well?" "Sir," the invalid replied, "I have no one to help me into the pool when the water is stirred. While I am trying to get in, someone else goes down ahead of me." Then Jesus said to him, "Get up! Pick up your mat and walk." At once, the man was cured. He picked up his mat and walked.

Here we have a man who has been an "invalid" or a person made weak or disabled by illness or injury for *thirty-eight years*. He lived in an environment where everyone had some sickness, and the only way they could be healed of their condition was by dipping themselves in the pool when the water was troubled. Can you imagine the conversations, agony, and depression that place witnessed? I would guess there was a lot of complaining and that victim mentality was running rampant. Granted, they did have illnesses with which they were dealing, and each person was so focused on their condition that they didn't prepare their minds to get to the water. At least this was the case for the invalid man. When I read the story, I heard the disappointment and saw he wanted to be healed. He told Jesus every time he tried to do it, someone would get in before him. Something stood out to me—he had been this way for thirty-eight years!

You mean to tell me you were tired of a condition, knew the water would be troubled soon, and you didn't stay by the pool? That tells me he grew comfortable in his state. That is why Jesus asked him, "Do you want to be made well?" Instead of giving him a yes or no answer, the invalid man made an excuse and had a pity party that no one had helped him. Luckily, Jesus saw beyond his response and healed him anyway.

Before this becomes judgmental, let me say I, too, had a victim mentality. When I was hurt as a child, all my mind wanted to do was go into survival mode. Therefore, I built walls to protect myself from "danger." I didn't realize those walls would keep me trapped for years. Then I began to love this space because it gave me the "excuse" to stay where I was. It helped me to avoid the fear of the unknown. If I do get healed, how would my life look? The victim mentality allowed me to stay in control. I'll never forget when I told one of my friends about what had happened to me as a child, he was very sympathetic and told me he was so sorry for what I went through. Then, he started seeing destructive behaviors and patterns in me that were stopping me from maturing in my walk with Christ. One day, he told me, "You are playing the victim to stay comfortable in pity. Get up and be healed!" *Ouch*! That hurt but it also helped my life.

The victim mentality provides three things for us: power, validation, and attention. It gives us power in the sense that we can control the narrative, and we can also manipulate people into doing things for us because of our "situation." When one has been wounded or abandoned, we want and need validation. The victim mentality's "validation" says it is acceptable to stay in this type of attitude. Why not? People are at your beck and call because they feel sorry for you. All this leads to a person receiving the *attention* they have always desired from childhood. Luckily, the victim mentality is a learned behavior that can be unlearned.

THE DECISION

Today is a crucial day for you because it requires making a firm decision. Before you answer too quickly, I want you to take in what I am about to explain. One of the thoughts that haunts me every day is when this life is all said and done, did I fully become who I was created to be?

Ask yourself this question now: If you were to leave earth tomorrow, what would die with you?

With that answer in mind, consider this question:

Will you make the decision today to be free and not waste any more time not living to your full potential as God created you to be?

Take a moment to think through your answer. If your honest answer is *no*, then that is your right to choose.

If your answer is *yes*, here's what it means:

Your world, as you know it, will never be the same. You're changing for the greater good, and it's hard. The firm decision to say *yes* gets you through the tough times when you want to give up because you have made the firm resolve you want better and will no longer settle.

Your decision to say *yes* will serve as a reminder when your past calls you to go back and be mediocre or live in bondage.

Your *yes* decision requires you to change as an individual, so you become better, a person of character and integrity.

Your *yes* gets you closer to your dreams and what you were created to be. It is a life filled with passion, purpose, and fulfillment.

Your *yes* makes you a warrior and protector of your destiny. When people and situations come to threaten your future, your determined mind won't allow them to sabotage anything.

Your *yes* allows others to see that it's possible for them, too. You have people who "knew you when," and when they see you, they will know there is something different about you now. The change comes as a result of internal change and the determination to move forward.

It is difficult to stop somebody who has made a firm decision to change and who has the resolve to stick to it. There comes a time when what is before you is greater than the desire to stay where you are.

I'm a huge Tyler Perry fan, and he and I have similar (almost identical) stories. He is someone who is a dreamer who became everything he was created to be. He wrote a play called *Madea Gets a Job* and created a character named Hattie. She is hilarious! In this particular play, she sang a song with lyrics that cause one to think about life every day. The song is called "Say."

In short, this is a story about a woman who is dropped off at a nursing home by her sister. She sits at the door and waits for someone to come back to pick her up, but no one shows up. She starts to reminisce and wonder how she is sitting there all alone after it seems like yesterday she was young and taking care of her children. Hattie tells the audience that life is but a moment, and it comes and go like the wind. Now she's old, her life is coming to an end, and she is all alone.

Wow! I ask you: "How much longer?"

How much longer are you going to allow the past to steal your future?

How much longer will you wake up each morning merely existing in life?

How much longer will you keep ignoring your dreams?

How much longer will you allow negative words to define you?

How much longer will you live with low self-esteem?

How much longer will you continue that cycle of addiction that's killing you on the inside?

How much longer will you put off becoming the person you were created to be?

How much longer will you go to a job you hate knowing you have businesses within you?

How much longer will you put off taking that vacation?

How much longer will you allow the fear of rejection to keep you from making that life-changing phone call?

How much longer will you put off practicing?

How much longer will you continue to be financially dependent?

How much longer will you stay in that abusive relationship?

How much longer will you continue to project an "image" when you are broken on the inside?

How much longer will you put off going back to school?

You make the choice today! Remember, you are making a firm decision either to stay right where you are or not to allow your past to hinder you so you can move forward. Your choice today will provide you with the life you always dreamed of or one full of regret.

5

TIME TO FACE IT

If you've made the decision not to let your past hinder your future, this next step is so crucial. Remember, the *yes* requires courage and takes you out of your comfort zone. What would you do if you were walking along minding your own business, and a bush called your name as it burst into flames? If you are anything like me, you would make like Usain Bolt and get out of there! Most people would say that it is a fictional story and could never happen. Well, that was not the case for a man named Moses, who had an interesting childhood. His encounter is told in Exodus 2 & 3 and details the next step in this journey.

Now a man of the tribe of Levi married a Levite woman, and she became pregnant and gave birth to a son. When she saw that he was a beautiful child, she hid him for three months. But when she could protect him no longer, she got a papyrus basket for him and coated it with tar and pitch. Then she placed the child in it and put it among the reeds along the bank of the Nile. His sister stood at a distance to see what would happen to him.

Then Pharaoh's daughter went down to the Nile to bathe, and her attendants were walking along the riverbank. She saw the basket among the reeds and sent her female slave to get it.

She opened it and saw the baby. He was crying, and she felt sorry for him. "This is one of the Hebrew babies," she said.

Then his sister asked Pharaoh's daughter, "Shall I go and get one of the Hebrew women to nurse the baby for you?"

"Yes, go," she answered. So the girl went and got the baby's mother. Pharaoh's daughter said to her, "Take this baby and nurse him for me, and I will pay you." So the woman took the baby and nursed him. When the child grew older, she took him to Pharaoh's daughter and he became her son. She named him Moses, saying, "I drew him out of the water."

One day, after Moses had grown up, he went out to where his people were and watched them at their hard labor. He saw an Egyptian beating a Hebrew, one of his people. Looking this way and that and seeing no one, he killed the Egyptian and hid him in the sand. The next day he went out and saw two Hebrews fighting. He asked the one in the wrong, "Why are you hitting your fellow Hebrew?"

The man said, "Who made you ruler and judge over us? Are you thinking of killing me as you killed the Egyptian?" Then Moses was afraid and thought, "What I did must have become known."

When Pharaoh heard of this, he tried to kill Moses, but Moses fled from Pharaoh and went to live in Midian, where he sat down by a well.

During that long period, the king of Egypt died. The Israelites groaned in their slavery and cried out. Their cry for help because of their slavery went up to God. God heard their groaning and he remembered his covenant with Abraham, with Isaac and with Jacob. So God looked on the Israelites and was concerned about them.

Now Moses was tending the flock of Jethro his father-in-law, the priest of Midian, and he led the flock to the far side of the wilderness and came to Horeb, the mountain of God. There the angel of the LORD appeared to him in flames of fire from within a bush. Moses saw that though the bush was on fire, it did not burn up. So Moses thought, "I will go over and see this strange sight—why the bush does not burn up."

When the LORD saw that he had gone over to look, God called to him from within the bush," Moses! Moses!"

And Moses said, "Here I am."

"Do not come any closer," God said. "Take off your sandals, for the place where you are standing is holy ground." Then he said, "I am the God of your father, the God of Abraham, the God of Isaac and the God of Jacob." At this, Moses hid his face because he was afraid to look at God.

The LORD said, "I have indeed seen the misery of my people in Egypt. I have heard them crying out because of their slave drivers, and I am concerned about their suffering. So I have come down to rescue them from the hand of the Egyptians and to bring them up out of that land into a good and spacious land, a land flowing with milk and honey—the home of the Canaanites, Hittites, Amorites, Perizzites, Hivites, and Jebusites. And now the cry of the Israelites has reached me, and I have seen the way the Egyptians are oppressing them. So now, go. I am sending you to Pharaoh to bring my people the Israelites out of Egypt."

But Moses said to God, "Who am I that I should go to Pharaoh and bring the Israelites out of Egypt?"

And God said, "I will be with you. And this will be the sign to you that it is I who have sent you: When you have brought the people out of Egypt, you will worship God on this mountain."

Moses said to God, "Suppose I go to the Israelites and say to them, 'The God of your fathers has sent me to you,' and they ask me, 'What is his name?' Then what shall I tell them?"

God said to Moses, "I AM WHO I AM. This is what you are to say to the Israelites: 'I AM has sent me to you.'"

One of the hardest things in life is to face the thing you have run from for a long time. Of course, nobody wants to be reminded of their shortcomings and past failures. That is the case with Moses' story as you read before, but you see how it ended. It takes courage to face your past. Let's take a look at the lessons from the story we must apply in our personal lives to move forward.

1. *Time to face your personal Pharaoh.* Ever since your birth, there has been a hit out on your life. That is why so many things have happened to you over the years. Pharaoh comes in different forms: anger, abuse, childhood wounds, and fresh wounds. The fear of facing Pharaoh can be overwhelming because it seems so big and unmanageable. The instinctive thing is to run and hide, but to move forward with who you were created to be you have to face the past fully. You have to ask yourself, *What or who is my personal Pharaoh? What has me in bondage? What have I been dealing with since birth or a young child that has stolen my life?* This Pharaoh is here to steal your future and take your identity. That is why you must identify the enemy, so you know who and what is the target. You also have to face and let go of the comfort of the Pharaoh. Moses lived with the very people that once tried to kill him and his people at birth. He took on the ways of the Egyptians, but it was not who he was. We as people have lived with our Pharaohs and pains too long. You must get away and detach yourself from such false security.

2. *Time to face the guilt.* It is easy to deny any allegations of wrongdoing when you are innocent, but it is tough to face the real truth that you are not innocent. As

you read in Moses' case, he was guilty because he had killed a man and thought no one had seen him. When his crime was exposed, he ran to Midian to hide for forty years. For all these years, it has been easy for you to run away and hide because of the guilt. Whether you abandoned your children, hurt a loved one, slept with someone else's spouse, had an addiction that caused strain to your immediate family, were caught in a scandal, or stole the money—there are many things you are guilty of, but the most crucial concept you must understand is that you still have purpose.

One of the best ways to combat guilt is to turn it from a negative situation to one of development. Guilt says you did something wrong, and it went against your moral code—this is good because it sets up boundaries and helps you to learn from your mistakes. Often the feeling of guilt alone makes one want to change, and this is where growth takes place. Guilt enables you to avoid making the same mistakes repeatedly—at least it is supposed to. Truly overcoming guilt requires accountability. It is always good to get another perspective because we may be too hard on ourselves and give ourselves an unfair "punishment."[2] Accountability also dispels secrecy, which is one of the leading causes of internal torment. You need to tell someone you trust why you are feeling guilty. You do not have a time machine, and you cannot go back and change the past. We would all love to have this luxury, but we don't. We do have the luxury of changing our futures. Do something different today to make your life better and go in a different direction. Guilt makes us sit in despair and mediocrity, but we deserve better. Hear me when I say this, my friend—let it go!

3. *Time to face the shame.* Shame is a touchy subject, but it's one that must be handled. First, we must understand the difference between guilt and shame. According to BetterHelp.com, guilt is defined as "an emotional state that comes when we feel we have failed to live up to our own or other's morals or standards. Guilt includes both thoughts of how we have failed and distressing emotions like sadness, anger, or anxiety. It continues to explain that shame is an intense feeling about the self that comes from failing to live up to your own or others' standards." [3] The main difference between guilt and shame is that with shame, you see yourself as a bad person rather than a good person who has done something terrible. Secondly, let's define the two types of shame—healthy and toxic shame. Healthy shame helps us to understand our limitations as human beings. It tells us when we have made a mistake that goes against our ideals or values. This type of shame shows us we need to rectify the situation to come into a better state of how we see ourselves. Toxic shame, as defined by John Bradshaw, creates beliefs that one's true self is flawed and defective, creating a false sense that one is a broken human being.[4] Toxic shame says, "I am a mistake." We see ourselves from the lens of a failure versus the lens of God. Toxic shame hinders you from progressing, and it too causes us to hide from reality. I am sure this is what Moses felt after committing the mistake of killing the Egyptian slave master. He thought it was doing justice because the slave master was doing someone else harm. Moses' internal thoughts or toxic shame may have sounded like, "I am a murderer" or "I am a bad man." If you are experiencing toxic shame, I highly recommend you see a professional therapist. They are educated

on the most effective methods to help you unpack shame. Shame is also dispelled through vulnerability and sharing because it thrives through secrecy.

4. *Time to face the false image.* Here is where we take off the mask. Trauma and pain have a way of telling us that we need to hide and protect ourselves from ever being hurt again. Shame and guilt will also make us create a false identity—one that we want people to love. Moses fled to Midian because of his murderous act and created a whole new life. He hid for forty years! No one knew who he was and what he had done. His self-imposed exile probably felt like peace to him externally, but there was likely some constant reminder internally that reminded him of who he "truly" was. Moses married, had kids, and worked for his father-in-law, but he still had this secret. There is no peace in having secrets. This area is so crucial because you have to give yourself permission to be the real you and be real with the people who love you. The pressure to perform and to keep up appearances gets too overwhelming for one person because you have to know which person to bring out in front of different people. Enough is enough. Take that mask off and acknowledge that you are hurting. Allow people in so those wounds can heal.

5. *Time to face the conflict of the calling.* Can you imagine seeing a burning bush that is not being consumed? That would freak me out, and I do not think I would have walked over there to it. However, Moses did because he heard someone calling his name. In the story, you can see that God did not bring up Moses' past. He told Moses that He heard the cry of His people, and He needed Moses to go tell Pharaoh

to let His people go. Moses is the one who had the conflict and doubt because his internal voice was saying how unworthy he was, and his qualifications did not match with what God was asking. There was an internal conflict. The same goes for you. You have to face the inner conflict that you are not worthy of a great calling because of your past mistakes. Let's throw that out the window now. You still have a purpose despite what you have done.

6. *Time to face the people.* I have to admit that this is one of the hardest things you will have to do, especially if you have struggled with people-pleasing or codependency. It takes boldness and assurance of who you are because you have to face the people who "knew you back when." Please understand you have no control of how the people will respond to you, and worrying about it is not your job. You are not the same person anymore, and you are not what you have done. Make that firm resolve today. You must understand, and obey, that you have been called and instructed by God to them. Walk boldly in that because these people will see the fruit through your actions and results. It says in the Word that a tree is known by its fruit. Therefore, people can bring up your past and who you use to be, but they cannot deny the change that has taken place in you because your fruit reveals all. What people may He be instructing you to return to? Is it the person who hurt you to say you forgive them? Is He asking you to give a donation or start a program for a struggling school in which you were teased? Are you to take care of a parent who abandoned you? You never know what the calling is or the people you will have to "set free," but know that it will help their life as well as yours.

For many years I ran from my past. I was too embarrassed and scared to acknowledge that there was a problem. One incident created a whole lot of issues in my life. The easy thing to do was run, hide, and pretend everything was okay, but healing can't take place like that. I gained the courage to acknowledge my "Pharaohs" finally. I had to face that I was molested as a child. I needed to confront lust and an addiction to pornography from the age of eleven, hear over and over the words said by people in school, acknowledge the fact that I felt abandoned and lonely most of my life due to the pain, and face the anger that I wanted my life to be normal, but it wasn't because of all the things that had happened to me. Depression, anxiety, codependency, and self-pity all wrecked my life. As mentioned in the previous chapter, this made me a victim and halted my life. Therefore, I had to face each of these things and tell them to let me go!

When I started seeing a professional therapist, he told me that I was dealing mostly with toxic shame. I had in my mind that I was a bad person and was unlovable and that God couldn't change or love a person like me. The counselor also helped me to take off the mask and gave me a safe place to be vulnerable and myself. It felt like the weight of the world was lifted off my shoulders because I was carrying something that weighed me down—a false identity. This journey required me to go back to places that I never wanted to go—back to those hurtful moments, to the people that hurt me, relationships where I had damaged some people. It was not easy, and I wanted to run away because that was my go-to response when things became hard.

It all made sense the day God showed me what He did for me. He vividly showed me that one day, when I was severely teased in junior high school outside of the choir room. An angel was shielding me from the darts of their words. These were very harsh words! I was so grateful for the vision because it showed that I was loved. My burning bush experience came when I was so low and deep in depression because of my pain and sin. That was when my mindset was that I could never be forgiven or loved because of my past. Then God showed me how he took my outer flesh and hung and nailed it to the cross where Jesus was. Then He held up a mirror, and there was no longer an image of me but of Christ. That's when I knew I had been forgiven and had the purpose of telling my story and helping other people.

Here's the truth: I have to stay in relationship and communion with God continually to keep on the right track. If there is no constant renewing of the mind through the Word, then I'm easily susceptible to living in my past. No one has time for that! It's a fight every day, but it's also a choice to stay free. One has to have a made-up mind that even though it's going to be hard, I'm willing to face whatever comes my way to try and hold me back from living the life I was promised.

6

THE LOUD LIES

"Bradley, come here for a second."

"Why are you whispering, Lori?"

"Because I don't want to wake up Eli. He hasn't been feeling too well, and he won't let me put him down."

"We've taken him to the doctor every day this week. Do you think the fever has something to do with the ear infection?"

"I don't know. The doctor said it would go away in a couple of days, but he's still hot."

"Well, it's Saturday, so let's see if Dr. Culpepper, the pediatrician, can see Eli today."

A whimper comes from Eli when he feels the vibrations from his mom's humming.

"Mommy, I'm thirsty. May I have some juice?"

"Of course you can, baby. Can Mommy put you down for a second to get it for you?"

"No, please don't put me down. Me not feeling too good."

Lori's eyes cut to Bradley, and with haste, the stocky, bearded man ran to start the car.

After arriving at the doctor's office, the family waits patiently in the exam room.

"Honey, I am so nervous. Look at our little boy," says Lori.

Young Eli, in his red Power Ranger pajamas, bear hugs his mom as he sweats from a fever.

"I know, babe. He's going to be just fine."

Out of nowhere, three knocks come on the heavy, brown, squeaking door.

"Hello, Grayson family. It's like I've seen you every day this week."

Lori nods her head and confirms, "Yes, it may seem that way, Dr. Culpepper."

"Hmmm...here's what I'd like to do. I want to get some blood work tested on Eli to see if it tells us anything about what's going on."

"Blood work?" asks Bradley.

"Yes, just a standard sample, which could reveal the cause for this fever and Eli's other symptoms."

"Do whatever you need to get our boy well, Doctor," says Bradley.

The nurses prepped all the needles and got the blood drawn from Eli—after a struggle and screams.

Hours passed by, and the Graysons couldn't seem to keep still until more knocks came from the door.

Dr. Culpepper's presence sent shock waves through their bodies.

"You'll need to go to the children's hospital immediately to see doctors there. There were a few things that we saw that are beyond our expertise and scope of work. I've already called the children's hospital, and you'll be seeing Dr. Gleason, the pediatric hematologist oncologist."

Panicked and concerned, the family packs up their things to get in the truck to head over to the hospital.

Upon arrival, they check in at the receptionist's desk, and the nurse said, "Oh, we are expecting you. Dr. Culpepper has already sent over the blood work tests, and Dr. Gleason is in the room waiting for you."

As they walk in, they are met by Dr. Gleason, his resident Matt, and nurse Chandra. Lori tightly hugs Eli and begins to cry.

"Please, ma'am, don't cry," Dr. Gleason affirms. "You are in great hands."

"Unfortunately, we do have some bad news. We need to admit Eli immediately to the children's hospital on floor six. I am very concerned because of the low blood count we're seeing in him. Other kids who have had this low red blood cell level were diagnosed ultimately with leukemia."

"*Leukemia?*" both parents blurt out in panic.

"Nurse Chandra will take you up to floor six and get Eli comfortable in a room," Dr. Gleason said.

The nurse brings in a wheelchair for Lori and Eli to sit in to take them upstairs.

It felt like years getting to the elevator because of devastation.

The bell from the elevator startled the husband and wife as it signaled they had arrived at floor six.

Rolling off the elevator, Lori immediately heard a voice, "Are you going to choose faith or fear?"

The question threw her off for a second, but Lori made up her mind that she was going to choose faith.

Immediately, negative voices started to bombard her mind as they traveled to their room.

"You see those little kids on the wall? That's going to be your son."

"Hey, Lori! Are you really going to choose faith? No way! Your son won't make it."

Lori reaches for Bradley's hand and begins to weep as they made it to the room.

The doctors run a few tests and hours pass.

Suddenly, they hear three bangs on the wooden, brown door. Time stood still as the door opened. It was Dr. Gleason.

44

"After running a few more tests, all three blood levels have dropped even more. That concerns us to the point that if it drops two more times, he is going to need a blood transfusion. We'll monitor Eli overnight."

"Okay, that sounds good," both parents agree nervously.

That night, Lori began to have bad dreams. Those little voices came back to torment her in her sleep.

"Ha-ha, you see everything is getting worse. Your faith is not going to work here. Just give in and know that your child has cancer."

Lori mumbles and tussles in her sleep, which triggered Bradley's reaction.

"Babe wake up. Lori, wake up!"

Gasping for air, Lori wakes up.

"That's it! We're about to fight," Lori yells.

"You must've heard those nagging voices too in your sleep, huh?" Bradley asks.

"Yes, and I am tired of them."

Bradley agrees, "Me, too. Well, let's fight!"

Bradley and Lori begin to write Scriptures on any paper they could find and taped them around the room.

Lori instructed, "We will only speak life and faith. Everything else is a lie, and we won't accept it. Our son does not have leukemia."

"I just got off the phone with Kimmie, and all our friends will be praying for Eli for twenty-four hours until he is healed."

"That's awesome," Bradley exclaims.

A few hours later, Dr. Gleason walks in the door.

"Wow, this room has really changed."

"Yes, it has. Do you have any good news for us, Doctor?" Lori asks.

"Unfortunately, I don't have any good news. Overnight, Eli's blood levels dropped again, and we would like for him to take part in our bone marrow study. The nurse has the waiver here for you to review and sign. Let me know if you have any questions."

Bradley reaches for the paperwork and says, "Thank you so much, Dr. Gleason. We will review this paperwork."

Bradley and Laurie look over the paperwork, but they are stopped in their tracks.

"Lori, look at this," Bradly whispers.

You have been chosen for this study because your child has been diagnosed with Acute Leukemia.

"Excuse me, Dr. Gleason," Bradley interrupts, "we won't be able to sign this."

"Why not?" Dr. Gleason asks.

"If we sign this, we are basically saying that our son has leukemia. We don't mind participating in the study, but there's no way we're signing this."

"Well, that document is required to participate in the study. It's best that you all sign."

Lori interjects, "I hear what you're saying, and we are not crazy. We are people of faith. We will use your wisdom as a doctor, but we cannot accept or sign-off on this diagnosis."

Dr. Gleason sits puzzled. "Okay. We will still need to go in and do some more tests on the bone marrow to determine what our next steps are and to see if any actual signs come back. Does that sound fair?"

Both parents agree.

"Before you take him back, can we pray for you and the entire team?" Bradley asks.

Everyone got in a circle and locked hands. Bradley begins to pray.

Nothing could prepare them for the long waiting time in the waiting room. However, Bradley and Lori were equipped with the Scriptures needed to ward off any negative voices.

Five hours pass by, and Dr. Gleason comes into the waiting room and says, "Everything went great with the procedure.

Eli is back in the room, so you are more than able to go back and see him. We'll want him to stay overnight to monitor him. He should be fine. We'll have results and an update for you tomorrow."

"Thank you so much," Bradley and Lori say as they pass Dr. Gleason—hurrying to get to their son.

Hearing the door opening, Eli cries out, "Mommy, Daddy. Where are you?"

Both parents affirm, "We're right here, Son."

"It hurts. I'm ready to go home." Eli tries to move, but pain halts him.

Lori rushes over, "No, Son, don't try to move. Here. Here's a popsicle for you."

The parents caress his head to comfort him.

By this time, Bradley and Lori's parents have made it into town, and are providing support for their kids.

They hear three knocks hit the door and in comes Dr. Gleason, Jared—a resident fellow, and Dr. Thompson—an attending physician.

"Bradley and Lori, we'd like to speak with you in private," Dr. Gleason instructs.

Immediately their stomachs drop to the bottom of their floor.

"Dr. Gleason, whatever you have to say, you can say it in front of the entire family. We're okay with that," Lori says firmly.

"Alright. We found a two percent blast in Eli's bone cells. However, they are not reproducing."

"Not reproducing," Lori asks. "What does this mean?"

They nervously await his response.

"Well, it means that Eli doesn't have leukemia, and we will be discharging him in an hour."

Bradley and Lori fell to the floor and began to weep and send up praises. They were elated about the news they had just received.

They hugged Eli as tears fell on the top of his head. An hour later, they left the hospital with a well child.

Eli's story is true! To make things even better, when Eli went for a checkup two weeks later, they could see no signs of cancer, and his blood work was significantly improved.

Awesome!

There are a few lessons in Bradley and Lori's story that are so crucial for us to understand as we are on the journey to wholeness and living a full life. The most important lesson is knowing our true identity.

When a person has been abused or traumatized, their identity is usually lost or stolen. We don't know who we are. We look for love and fulfillment in all the wrong places: sex, people, success, drugs, money, or notoriety. These acts are a byproduct of emptiness in the soul. Another aspect of being abused is that we always believe the worst about ourselves and situations. These are called lies, and they happen in the mind.

It must be noted—and you should fully understand—that you have an adversary whose job is to lie to you every chance he gets. He plays on secrets, lies, worry, and anxiety. These lies may be any of the following: you're ugly, you're not worthy, you will never be enough, you are nothing without success, your dreams will never come true, you will always be poor, no one can love you, your wife doesn't love you, or you will never be a good husband.

These seem like our thoughts and voices, but they really aren't.

These lies may have been believed for years, so they play over and over in the mind—even without you paying attention to them. Anything we feel for so long we make a part of who we are.

Do you remember in the story when Eli was showing signs of cancer? That was the truth. The doctors saw it in his blood work. However, Eli's parents did not accept the diagnosis because they believed God who said their child was healed and whole in His Word. What does this mean for you? Even if something is true or you are guilty of an act, you don't have to accept the label or identity arising from that mistake.

For years, I didn't know why I would keep going in vicious cycles of weight gain, addiction, depression, and selfish ambition. The moment I said I wouldn't do something, I'd be triggered to do that very thing. That was because I believed the lies about myself carried over from when I was an abused child. As mentioned before my counselor told me that I was dealing with toxic shame. Ultimately, I was believing lies in my mind (and heart) that I was unlovable and damaged because of what had happened to me. When I went to see one of my mentors, I shared with him all the things I was experiencing and feeling. It was a complaining session for which I'm sure he wasn't ready. He became quiet and gave me one of the most serious looks I've ever seen. His head shook back and forth, and he began to weep. He said, "You don't know who you are and how powerful you are. You don't know your identity in Christ."

In the back of my mind and being religious for so many years, I thought he wasn't telling the truth because I knew who I was. In actuality, I knew what the Word said about who I was, but I didn't believe it in my heart. There is a difference between head knowledge and heart knowledge. I tried to keep up the façade on the outer, but my internal struggles and beliefs were saying something way different. Just like Bradley and Lori, I had to learn how to fight, which required me to take every lie in my head and trade it for the truth of God's Word in my heart. It had gotten to such a point of desperation (and after watching the movie *War Room*) that I cleaned out my master closet and turned it into a prayer room. I posted notecards around it on which I wrote Scriptures describing who I was in Christ and areas of where I needed truth. Anytime I would have overwhelming thoughts of lies, I would run to my "secret place" to be surrounded by the truth of who I am. It wasn't enough to run to that place, but I also meditated and visualized those truths so I could see who I was.

Today, I am saying to some of you, "You don't know who you are. You don't know your identity in Christ." I'm also announcing today that you will learn how to fight because the nagging voices are playing on some "truths" (mistakes), but that is not who you are.

Here's an activity I'd like you to do. You don't necessarily have to turn your entire closet into a prayer room, but take a sheet of paper, divide it down the middle, and write down the nagging voices and lies that come to mind or what you believe about yourself. One column should be labeled *Lies*, and the other side should be labeled *Truths*. Here's an example:

Lies	Truths
I feel ugly and unlovable.	I am fearfully and wonderfully made.
	I am loved by God because He first loved me.
I don't have a purpose.	I am a chosen person, a royal priesthood, a holy nation, God's special possession.

When doing this exercise, I want you to write your *Truths* in "I am" and "affirmation" form. Your truths should also come from the Word of God. We need something that has power over the lies of the adversary, and the Word is just like a sword. Anytime a lie bombards your mind or tries to make you feel unworthy, you must say the truth out loud. In some instances, you'll have to keep saying it until the lie dissolves.

Our greatest teacher of this principle is Jesus. When the devil tempted Jesus in the wilderness, Jesus had to say the Word back to the devil constantly in Matthew 4:1-11:

> Then Jesus was led by the Spirit into the wilderness to be tempted by the devil. After fasting forty days and forty nights, he was hungry. The tempter came to him and said, "If you are the Son of God, tell these stones to become bread."
>
> Jesus answered, "It is written: 'Man shall not live on bread alone, but on every word that comes from the mouth of God.'"
>
> Then the devil took him to the holy city and had him stand on the highest point of the temple. "If you are the Son of God," he said, "throw yourself down. For it is written:
>
> "'He will command his angels concerning you, and they will lift you up in their hands, so that you will not strike your foot against a stone.'"
>
> Jesus answered him, "It is also written: 'Do not put the Lord your God to the test.'"
>
> Again, the devil took him to a very high mountain and showed him all the kingdoms of the world and their splendor. "All this I will give you," he said, "if you will bow down and worship me."
>
> Jesus said to him, "Away from me, Satan! For it is written: 'Worship the Lord your God and serve him only.'"
>
> Then the devil left him, and angels came and attended him.

You are an amazing individual and are loved by the Father. It is hard to stop somebody who knows who they are. There's a confidence that exudes from that person, and they don't get caught up in things that do not pertain to their destiny and God-given identity. It may take a little while, but eventually, you will start walking in who you are. You don't have to accept any lie told by the enemy. Remember, your words have power, so say your truths out loud.

7

HEALING FOR THE JOURNEY

When I moved to Nashville in 2012, I learned the valuable lessons mentioned in the last chapter. I started interning with Warner Music Group, one of the largest record labels in the world and worked for a company that promoted the top faith-based films around the country. All my life, I had wanted to work in the entertainment industry, sing around the world, and be in productions. Moving to Nashville felt like I had hit the jackpot, and all of my dreams were going to come true all in one moment—or so I thought. My dreams were not coming true fast enough, and I needed to help them come to fruition more quickly. However, the more I tried to make these things happen, the more frustrated I became. Doors began to close, and opportunities started to dry up. Long-term relationships began to be strained, my reputation became questionable, and I found myself in a very dark place. Disappointment and discouragement were dark clouds hovering over my life.

At that time, I decided I needed to take a break from "chasing" my dreams because I was so burned out, broke, depressed, and I had little hope of achieving my goals. To avoid becoming homeless, I had to get a job. I hated that three-letter word. Why? It went against the image I was trying to portray—a young, successful entrepreneur who worked in the music, television and film industry. A job would also take away my freedom and the ability to work from the comfort of my own home while pursuing my dreams. It was not a joyous occasion, and I had to ask myself, why were these things happening? It was not until I came across the story in Joshua 5:1-9 that I began to understand.

> Now, when all the Amorite kings west of the Jordan and all the Canaanite kings along the coast heard how the LORD had dried up the Jordan before the Israelites until they had crossed over, their hearts melted in fear and they no longer had the courage to face the Israelites.
>
> At that time the LORD said to Joshua, "Make flint knives and circumcise the Israelites again." So Joshua made flint knives and circumcised the Israelites at Gibeath Haaraloth.
>
> Now this is why he did so: All those who came out of Egypt—all the men of military age—died in the wilderness on the way after leaving Egypt. All the people that came out had been circumcised, but all the people born in the wilderness during the journey from Egypt had not. The Israelites had moved about in the wilderness forty years until all the men who were of military age when they left Egypt had died, since they had not obeyed the LORD. For the LORD had sworn to them that they would not see the land he had solemnly promised their ancestors to give us, a land flowing with milk and honey. So he raised up their sons in their place, and these were the ones Joshua circumcised. They were still uncircumcised because they had not been circumcised on the way. And after the whole nation had been circumcised,

they remained where they were in camp until they were healed.

Then the LORD said to Joshua, "Today I have rolled away the reproach of Egypt from you." So the place has been called Gilgal to this day.

Here we have a story about the children of Israel who were just about to crossover to the Promised Land. They were excited because what God promised their parents would finally come to fruition. However, a wrench was thrown into their parade because Joshua came with an announcement that probably shocked them. "All men, you have to be circumcised before you cross over." I'm sure they responded with "What? Circumcision?" That meant more pain for them after a forty-year journey. They were through with pain, but they had to oblige. Why? Because it was a requirement to see the Promised Land. Circumcision involves the cutting away of the male's foreskin and undergoing the procedure showed they were in covenant with God. He knew the health benefits of circumcision, but He also knew cutting away the unnecessary flesh would allow them to reproduce life.

The key point from the story in this chapter is they remained where they were in camp until their surgical wounds were healed. That's right. They had to wait a little while longer before going over to the Promised Land because they needed to recover from the cutting and pain of circumcision.

Aha! It all made sense now in my personal life—I needed to get rid of all the junk in my heart that was hindering me. I could not identify those things because I was always oblivious to the reality of my actual state. The pursuit of my "dreams" was a way to avoid the pain I was feeling. It was time to allow the cutting and healing process to start. So, I got a job.

The job was as the Director of First Impressions at Keller Williams—a real estate company. It was a great title, and it fed my pride to have it, but the truth is I was a glorified secretary. I had come through a temp agency, and by the end of the week, the CEO offered me the position full-time. In my head, I had already said no. It was not until I had a phone call with a friend who told me I should take the position that I reconsidered.

"Isiah, you're broke. This would provide some stability, consistency, income, benefits, and new relationships. Humble yourself and see what God does." I wanted to hang up the phone in her face, but deep down inside, I knew this is what I needed to do. I accepted the position.

To my surprise, the "job" would open my eyes to the areas that were hindering my growth. Here are a few areas that needed some attention: pride, laziness, entitlement, lack of character, and lying. It all was a shock to me because I believed I was the "golden child," but that title was about to be tested.

There were over 250 agents in that office who loved coffee. A part of my job was cleaning up the coffee machine, washing dishes, and replenishing a candy bowl several times a day. Performing those duties was like eating a big slice of humble pie for me because I thought I was too good to clean up after grown adults. The lesson God was trying to teach me was humility and a real sense of serving others. Did I mention I was consistently late several times a week? My boss would get on me because I didn't have the enthusiasm to do a job in which I felt trapped. Many people identify with this feeling today. I wanted to spread my wings and be free! I would always use the excuse traffic was terrible, or there was a wreck on the freeway. However, one can only use those excuses so many times. After being reprimanded several times, I got convicted and wanted to honor my commitment.

Being at the desk allowed my eyes to be open to new opportunities as well. Every week, I would have to go down a list to ensure all the homes that were under contract were still closing. There was a column with the agents' commission, and I was floored. I said to myself, "The agents are making my annual salary in three closings. What am I doing behind the desk?" After several months as the front desk person, I got my license to become a real estate agent. I was so excited! One stipulation made clear to me was that I could not accept any leads—potential clients—that came through the phone because that would create an unfair advantage for me related to the other agents in the office, and those leads belonged to a special council in the office.

I was disobedient and started talking to a lead who called one day looking for an agent. I thought I could get away with it, but that lead had called the office to ask about me as an agent. When the leadership team received the call from the lead asking for references, my boss was shocked and felt betrayed. I got convicted and felt guilty about speaking to the lead out of turn, so I called him back and explained that my position didn't allow me to take on clients. I pointed him in the direction to a more experienced agent. Then I received a text from my boss telling me to be at the office first thing in the morning. It made me nervous because I had a feeling of what was going on even though I wasn't exactly sure. That morning, I made it there, and the CEO walked into the office and didn't make eye contact with me. The CEO called me into his office with a letterhead upside down on the table. My boss was in tears and distraught. I could tell something was about to go down—me. They asked a few questions about the lead, and I told them the situation and what I did to rectify the wrongdoing. A sigh of relief seemed to flood the room because the firm's policy ordinarily required termination. My job was saved, and the CEO and my boss gave me a second chance. Gratefully, I was able to earn their trust! This episode was an important lesson on character for me. More than anything, I felt so bad in how I betrayed the trust of my boss. My behavior was a deep hurt in her heart that she told me disturbed her sleep and peace the day before. I never wanted to make anyone feel like that ever again.

Honestly, these were hard lessons to learn, but they were necessary. These character flaws had to be circumcised from my heart, or it would have destroyed any chance of me getting to the promised land. This particular healing process took seven months, after which I was able to leave the front desk to become a full-time agent. I found a new respect for life, and I had never experienced peace and joy like that before. My real estate business took off, and I became one of the top-producing individual agents in the office.

Throughout my healing process, I learned four lessons from Joshua 5:1-9 that helped me to understand why lying, pride, laziness, lack of character, and entitlement needed to be cut away.

You must learn to rest in God. At the beginning of this chapter, the kings (enemies) were afraid of the children of Israel because the kings had heard all the miracles God was doing for the children of Israel and how He was fighting for them. Fear crept into the kings' hearts because they knew they could not defeat the children of Israel if God were on their side. All the children of Israel had to do was rest in God and know that He would make ways for them that were unavailable to the ordinary person. In the next step of your journey, you will be going to an unknown place, and that can be scary within itself. That was my feeling of going to Keller Williams—it was a place that was unknown, and I did not want to be there. However, you have to trust God enough to know that He brought you to this place and that He has made ways for you that no other man could do. Take heart in knowing that if you rest in God, he will take care of everything and anything that tries to hinder you.

Obedience is the determining factor in experiencing the promise. During this time of rest, you will learn the voice of God, and you must do what He says precisely. The reason why the first generation of the Israelites did not get to see their promised land was that they were disobedient. They did what they wanted and suffered the consequences. Think about that. All the suffering they had to endure, being chased by Pharaoh and other incidents, and they still didn't get to see land? That is wasted time and life. Even Joshua took heed to the directions that were given to him. Although circumcision would be uncomfortable and painful, he knew it was a requirement to receive the promise that had been given years ago. In your case, that is why healing is so important. The cutting away of disobedience has to be finished in your life before you can move forward. During healing is the time when you will be challenged with either doing things your way or God's way. Choose God's way and endure the pain of the cutting because it is for your good. Obedience also builds character. When you are becoming who you were created to be, it is a must that you exemplify character. That means you are not one person behind closed doors and another on when you are in front of people. Because your calling requires you to be a leader, there's a requirement that this is worked out in you before you start leading. Think about all the areas of your life that may be conflicting with God's word and what He's telling you to do. Fall in line. Change. Just obey!

Healing shows you who you are and why you deserve the promise. In the story above, it stated: For the LORD had sworn to them that they would not see the land he had solemnly promised their ancestors to give us, a land flowing with milk and honey. So he raised up their sons in their place, and these were the ones Joshua circumcised. Some people who came before you did not get to experience the fullness of their lives because they missed their turns. Do not get me wrong. A person who is sixty-four years old can fulfill the purpose for which they were created. However, their purpose may look a little different when it is time to see the finished work. You have learned that disobedience is the reason why this happens often, and fear can be a significant factor as well, which can sometimes be attributed to non-belief. That is why healing from the cutting away of disobedience is paramount because during this time of healing you will get a clear understanding of who you are in Christ, which ultimately reveals you are a son or daughter of God. That is what is meant by "God raised" their sons. When someone raises another, that means they are teaching that person valuable lessons to ensure the student grows into a model individual. Ideals, character, and ways of thinking are passed down from the person doing the raising. The same goes here with God raising you and teaching you the valuable lessons needed for the promised land of your purpose. Take this time to reflect on the lessons God has been teaching you and how to apply it with an understanding that God gave these promises just for you.

Healing lets you know God is not disappointed in you. In the last part of the story, God told the children of Israel that "He has rolled away the reproach of Egypt from them." According to the dictionary, reproach means to address someone in such a way as to express disapproval or disappointment. Because of the first generation's disobedience, God reproached them. I am sure the children, as they were growing up, saw how disobedience—which angered God—impacted their parents' lives. If the children saw or heard their parents say God is mad at them, then the children take on that notion that God is angry at them, too. Sometimes our pasts have a way of telling us we are no good or we do not deserve God's love. We feel as if God is forever mad at us because of our past mistakes. That is not the case here because taking the time to heal allows you to decipher through all the lies and understand the nature of God. You must know that God is not mad at or disappointed in you. He is grateful for you and excited for you to experience everything He has promised you. When you are fully healed, the things of Egypt won't hinder or bother you anymore. You are also not reminded of the pain that once held you hostage. You may still see the scars from the battle, but you are not that person anymore. Walk confidently in knowing you are free, and you have a very big God rooting for you to win.

Throughout this journey, God wants to cut away all the "flesh" that has been hindering you from experiencing the life He created you to have. Just think about it. He wants to cut away the anger, shame, guilt, addictions, eating disorder, diseases, suicidal thoughts, and anything you can think of that have had you in a dark place. Why? Because you are a child of promise. The same covenant God had with the Children of Israel is the same promise He will keep with you.

Never neglect the healing process. It is necessary for the upcoming journey. Stay low and humble and do what you need to do to heal. You will thank yourself later, and it will lead you to the path for which you were created. So, heal now.

8

WHY YOU NEED TO LIVE

I wanted to take the time out to say congratulations! You made it! You fought long and hard, and the hard work finally paid off. You are now coming into the place of who you were created to be. Many people do not get to this part of life, and that is why you are different and unique. A new fight has just begun, and that is why you needed to heal and rest before moving forward. You're probably thinking, *I thought all the fighting and hard work was finished?* I wish that were the case, but there are "giants" where you are about to go, and you need to be equipped to defeat them. Here is an excellent example in Luke 17: 11-19.

> It happened that as he made his way toward Jerusalem, he crossed over the border between Samaria and Galilee. As he entered a village, ten men, all lepers, met him. They kept their distance but raised their voices, calling out, "Jesus, Master, have mercy on us!"
>
> Taking a good look at them, he said, "Go, show your-selves to the priests."
>
> They went, and while still on their way, became clean. One of them, when he realized that he was healed, turned

around and came back, shouting his gratitude, glorifying God. He kneeled at Jesus' feet, so grateful. He couldn't thank him enough—and he was a Samaritan.

Jesus said, "Were not ten healed? Where are the nine? Can none be found to come back and give glory to God except this outsider?" Then he said to him, "Get up. On your way. Your faith has healed and saved you."

Here we have ten lepers who were outcasts because of their disease. They saw a person who could help them, and he did. The directive to them was to show themselves to the priest. But why would they show themselves to the priest if they hadn't been healed yet? I believe it was merely obedience because of immense faith. To be reintroduced back into society, the priest would have to review and see there was no leprosy present. They rejoined their families and careers if they were cleared. However, Jesus asked them to take this step of faith before their healing was complete.

You must know your healing will continue as you move forward and share your story. The healing we saw in the previous chapter was to ensure that everything toxic from your past was cut away so that it would not destroy the place of promise. Healing is a life-long process, and it doesn't happen overnight. Therefore, you will see your healing continuously taking place as you decide to move forward with your life and live. Healing also takes place as you continually move forward with an attitude of gratitude. Thankfulness from yesterday's victories propels you forward and fuels your faith to face any future giants and helps you win future battles. Remembering the God who helped you in the past will also help you in the present and the future.

If walking into purpose and achieving your dreams were easy, everyone would be doing it. There's a price you have to pay, and there is a mindset you must have to win. Please note this fight is a little different. You are fighting from a place of rest.

How? God is with you, and He promised you this land! He will fight for you. He promised you this life—one full of peace, love, happiness, and abundance. Everything you have endured and experienced up until this point was preparation for this moment. Yes! What seemed like torture, abuse, hurt, shame, etc. were muscle-builders you will be able to utilize in this new place.

Let these nuggets be in the forefront of your mind as you move forward into purpose. So, when the going gets tough—which it will—and doubt tells you to run back to the comfortable, know these are the reasons why you must keep going forward.

God created you for this specific moment in time. He knew what you possessed on the inside, and all the gifts and talents would be needed right now—for this moment. Your birth date and the year was not a coincidence. It was strategically planned. Think about all the people in history who were great. What they created and what they did was paramount and still has an impact on us today. Martin Luther King, Jr., George Washington Carver, Bill Gates, Nelson Mandela, Albert Einstein, Mozart, Harriet Tubman, Oprah Winfrey, Dr. Mae Jemison, and a host of others. Do you get where I am going here? I'm pretty sure they suffered and had to endure some hard times, but they persevered, and their legacies continue. That goes for you, too. You will leave a legacy of impact and change. I want you to grasp this because you will not be one of the ones who have regrets or should haves, could haves, would haves on your death bed. Time is one thing we do not get back. Once it is spent, it is gone. This moment is so crucial because you are so needed in this time and era. Please know that. The names mentioned above probably didn't know who they were to become growing up.

However, something on the inside guided them to decide to be great and to take advantage of their moment. What if they had said no? We would not know about them today, and the world would probably be different. Could society still go on? Absolutely. However, the world would not be the same without them. With that being said, please do not miss your moment!

Your life is connected to the freedom of others. That is right! You can no longer live your life selfishly. When people see you thriving and living your dreams, it will spark the question: What does he or she have that I don't have? You'll be an inspiration and bring glory back to God. Also, what you have been given to do will be the outlet for many individuals to find their way to freedom. Your ideas will ignite passion in others and help put their lives on a new trajectory. This world needs your light! The person that immediately comes to mind is Harriet Tubman. She was nicknamed "Moses" because she helped to free many slaves. Her story will forever be told because she gave up her life for the freedom of others. She found a route to freedom and then went and rescued others. That is exactly what we are supposed to do. Go into the world and be great. While doing that, go out and make others great as well. Encourage people and give them the tools that helped you to become the person you are today. Life is so much fulfilling when your life helps others.

You deserve every great thing that is about to happen to and for you. Own this right now. Please hear me say you are not entitled to these things. It will require hard work, but because you put in the work, you deserve to be and see the places you are about to go. Get your passport if you have not already done so. You will see the world because you are a world-changer. Practice your speech for when you receive the Nobel Peace Prize. It is possible! All of these fantastic things are what you have been praying for all these years. Now your prayers are being answered. Do not shrink back into fear but go full force knowing you deserve this. My grandfather always told me: "Preparation will one day meet opportunity. The thing is, will you be ready?" That question stuck with me for years and even to this day. All your hard work will pay off and meet opportunity, and guess what? You will be ready! Take peace in knowing that.

You know who you are. Stop for a moment and let that sink in. You know who you are! This world is so lost and searching for a lot of things due to emptiness and past hurt. You can relate to this, but you don't "identify" with it any longer. When you walk into a room, you will shift the atmosphere because you exude confidence, and people will immediately know you are different. If you are faced with a decision that will compromise your integrity, you shut it down quickly and move on. When you know who you are, you can be truthful about where you've come from and excited about where you are going. Identity also takes the pressure off you to perform. You don't have to perform in this new place. Just walk in who you are, and everything else will follow suit. Remember, God has given you every place the sole of your foot touches. Why? Because your identity shows you that you are His child.

Hopefully, this chapter ignites a fire in you. As mentioned, keep these reasons in front of you, especially when times get rough. I cannot stress this enough. Now, let the real work begin!

9

DREAM AGAIN

One of the greatest feelings in the world is when a father surprises his son or daughter with a gift. A series of feelings and emotions go through his body as he anticipates his child's response: nervousness, anxiousness, excitement. He has always dreamed of the day where he is finally able to give this gift to his child. To make things even more exciting, he hides the gift in a secret place where only he knows where it is hidden.

When the child arrives home, he sees his father waiting at the door for him. He questions what he's up to, but the father is too giddy to speak. He lets his son know he has a gift for him, and he needs to find it. Without hesitation, the child immediately throws his backpack on the ground and searches around the house for the gift. The child looks high and low, turns over the furniture, runs to the garage, looks in the outdoor shed, runs upstairs to his room to look in his closet, and asks his little brother if he knows where it is. After a daunting search, the boy becomes fatigued, and the father no longer hears him moving. The father searches for the boy and finds him asleep on the floor. He became so tired that he stopped his search and never got the gift that day. The father was disappointed because the gift was in his hand, but the child never asked him where it was.

We see this scenario play out every single day in our lives. What do you mean? I'm so glad you asked! When we think of dreams, we think of what we have seen. Children think *I want to be a pilot. I want to be a doctor. I want to be rich. I want to be a famous singer. I want to be in the NBA.* All these aspirations are great, but I want to draw your attention to something. Many people achieve their dreams and live the lives they have dreamed of living. They have the glitz and the glamour, riches, fame, access, and status. You name it, and they have it! Innately, we are prone to desire those things based on the false illusion and among other things.

Here is a way to bring it home:

Oscar-Winning Comedian, Dies at 63 by Apparent Suicide
Actor Dies of Accidental Drug Overdose at Sober Living Center, Coroner Says
Singer Hospitalized for Mental Health Treatment After Reported Emotional Breakdown

These are actual headlines that sent a shock through people around the world. Some people chase after success because of emptiness or the lack of a sense of purpose. I am sharing these headlines because it is essential to understand the difference between a worldly dream and a Godly dream. Let's take a look at the difference. Earthly dreams will never bring internal satisfaction. These types of goals are rooted in selfish ambition and come with pressure to perform and be someone you are not. Worldly dreams bring temporary pleasure, and all the glory and focus is on the individual. There is a lack of fulfillment with this type of dream that can be achieved by only one person. It has the propensity to overwhelm a person, leaves the individual feeling worthless if the dream is not realized, and a lot of time is wasted. The person may feel lonely, may experience addictions, or have no sense of self. There is a high rate of jealousy and envy, which leads to an attitude of getting there by any means necessary, even if it means undercutting someone. Worldly dreams are rooted in pride, and one's legacy can be tainted with scandal. We want to avoid this at all costs.

Godly dreams, on the other hand, are the exact opposite: they bring internal and external satisfaction and are rooted in purpose. Godly dreams make the person feel fulfilled, and it takes faith and total reliance on God to make them come true. These dreams leave a positive legacy generation after generation. They're *big*. They help to change the lives of many people, impact the culture, are rooted in humility and serv-anthood, bring change to the world and peace to one's life, and are surrounded by favor, yet they still require hard work.

Let me draw your attention to this promise—"Delight yourself in the Lord, and He will give you the desires of your heart" (Psalm 37:4). At the beginning of this chapter, I mentioned some dreams we often hear people striving for—NBA player, supermodel, a doctor, entrepreneur, etc. Please know there is nothing wrong with worldly success and achieving great things. The idea of these dreams gets tainted when worldly success takes us down the wrong path. That's why motives are so important, and you must regularly re-evaluate them. The first part of that promise directs us to delight ourselves in the Lord. When you take delight in someone, you enjoy their company and listen to what he or she says. In this case, we delight ourselves in His word and spend time with Him. When we get to know Him, we become like Him. Therefore, we learn who we are and develop the capacity for what we desire. After we have proven ourselves trustworthy and our motives are shown to be pure, then He gives us the desires of our hearts. Also, this ensures we do not waste any time. You've heard it repeatedly said that when someone is assembling a product, and they do it by themselves without following the directions, then the product is put together, but it doesn't function properly. The manufacturer put those instructions in the box for a reason—they created the product. The same goes for God. Did you know before you were born that you were already designed to do something? Let me prove it to you:

> For we are his workmanship, created in Christ Jesus for *good works, which God prepared beforehand, that we should walk in them.* (Ephesians 2:10)

> *"For I know the plans I have for you,"* declares the LORD, "plans to prosper you and not to harm you, plans to give you hope and a future." (Jeremiah 29:11)

> I praise you because I am fearfully and wonderfully made; your works are wonderful, I know that full well. My frame was not hidden from you, when I was made in the secret place when I was woven together in the depths of the earth. *Your eyes saw my unformed body; all the days ordained for me were written in your book before one of them came to be.* (Psalm 139: 14-16)

When I found these promises, it made me leap for joy because I don't have to waste any more time searching or asking, *Why was I put on this earth?* It's already been lined out for me because the Creator prepared the good works beforehand. All I have to do is walk in them. The same goes for you, too. You no longer have to wander or wonder what you're supposed to be doing. When He promised that He would give us the desires of our hearts, He meant that. So, if you want to sing and have the gift of singing—sing. However, it just won't be any type of song, but it'll be the type that brings change. If you want to be a doctor—become a doctor. Your motives are purified from just wanting to make millions of dollars, but instead, you want to find the cure for cancer and use those millions of dollars to help support families with medical bills. Do you see where I am going with this?

Let's put this in a step by step system:

1. Find a peaceful place to pray, journal, and ask God, "What good works did you prepare for me beforehand that I should walk in them?"

2. Identify the gifts and talents you already possess or the dreams in your heart that you'd like to come true

3. Close your eyes and visualize yourself living your dreams

4. Write down what you see and feel

5. Put these questions to your dreams and what you saw in #4 to these questions:

   i. Does it glorify God?

   ii. Will it affect change in the world or people's lives? Bring souls to the Kingdom?

   iii. Does it line up with God's Word

6. If the answer is YES to all the questions in #5, then GO for it!

7. Ask God for clear direction (read Psalm 119:105)

   i. How are you (God) going to accomplish this?

  ii. What's my first step? The first step of faith will open the door to the next ones

  iii. Who are the people that are supposed to help me?

 8. Do the work required to accomplish God's dream (see Chapter 10)

Here are a few examples:

Aspiration: I desire to be a pilot.
 Godly Dream: I want to own a fleet of planes to fly people around the world for missions or gift families who can't afford vacations a chance to see the world.

Aspiration: I desire to be an entrepreneur.
 Godly Dream: I would like to provide jobs to felons who society says don't deserve a second chance.

Aspiration: I want to be a cosmetologist.
 Godly Dream: I would like to transform the lives of battered women whose self-esteem was destroyed from their previous relationship and restore their confidence in themselves again because they are beautiful.

 This chapter is titled "Dream Again" for a reason. We all have had dreams since we were young. Now that we know God has goals for our lives, we have to "dream again" to gain His perspective on what those dreams should look like and how it will change this world. You should be excited now because the pressure should be lifted. Many people's lives are halted by the question: "Why was I put on this earth?" You don't need to be that person anymore. Spend more time with the Creator (the manufacturer), and He will show you what you're supposed to be doing (the directions). Once

He shows you, then do it. I also want to let you know God doesn't want us to live boring and unfulfilled lives. He is the good Father that takes pleasure in seeing His children open the gifts He placed on the inside of them. Do not second guess that any longer. Any time that question as to whether you are supposed to be doing something arises, go back to the above test. Then have some fun changing this world! We can't waste any more time. We have to make up for the time that was lost all these years wandering around aimlessly in fear. It's time to put in the work!

10

DREAMS REQUIRE MUCH WORK

Congratulations! You have made it to another milestone and hopefully, have a better understanding of who you are and why you were placed on this earth. Many people associate their work as their nine to five, but in actuality, that is their job. Your true work is what you were created to do—your purpose. Now that you know this, it is time to go to *work*!

In Habakkuk 2:2, it says "And the LORD answered me: 'Write the vision; make it plain on tablets, so he may run who reads it.'"

Let's break this Scripture into pieces to understand the importance of writing the vision. First, it is crucial to get the concept out of your head and write it down on actual paper. When the idea remains in your mind, it is just a dream, which probably won't happen. However, if you write it down, it becomes real. There is a saying that goes straight to the heart of writing down your vision:

> "A dream written down with a date becomes a goal. A goal broken down into steps becomes a plan. A plan backed by action makes your dreams come true." [5]

It is okay to have a dream, but the world is changed by individuals who make their dreams reality. Breaking the dream down into goals and deadlines makes it more tangible. Steve Harvey says, "If you can see it in your mind, then you can hold it in your hands." I love it! We can take that even further by saying to hold it in our hands, we have to see it in our minds, write it down on paper, and get after it.

Make it plain on tablets is the next directive. Purchase a vision book—it can be a journal or tablet of your choosing. I'm a huge advocate of journals because writing is very freeing, and it allows you to express yourself when you can't necessarily articulate what you want to say out loud. However, this particular journal is for your ideas. Ideas can change your life because they usually solve a problem. Your vision is a solution to a problem. Take this vision book everywhere you go and lay it beside your bed every night. The moment an idea comes to you, write it down immediately. By keeping the journal with you, you will have all your ideas in one place.

Secondly, writing the vision brings clarity to the direction you are going. What we do not want to happen is that you spend more years wandering and asking what it is we are supposed to be doing. Getting clarity takes time because you have to ask yourself, *What is the actual vision?* We are no longer people wandering aimlessly, but instead, individuals who are confident and know where they are going. Saying you want to own a non-profit won't suffice. You have to say, "I want to create a non-profit by December 31ˢᵗ, (YEAR) called (NAME) where we help individuals (PURPOSE). (NAME) will build a shelter for the homeless that houses 130 people per night. The non-profit has twelve board members, and this is a list of individuals I would love to take part." The detail makes it clear and unambiguous. It requires much thought, but this time is worth it because it allows you to get to work faster. It also helps with the next component.

So he may run who reads it. The purpose of having and writing your vision down is for legacy. That is right. One of our goals should be to leave a legacy for the generations to come. It is backed by this Scripture, "A wise man leaves an inheritance for his children's children." (Proverbs 13:22a). Our impact is going to be so large that our children's children benefit from our dreams. Wow! Let that marinate. Each one of us has an expiration date. None of us are immortal. That is why your vision book is so important. Picture yourself on your death bed, and you are surrounded by your children. You and your children are sharing memories and laughing about the good old days. As a parting gift, you ask one of your children to open the drawer and get your vision book out. You instruct them to do what is in it *exactly*, and they would be taken care of for the rest of their lives. Do you get the picture? Now get to writing those details.

DISTRACTIONS

Another reason why you need to write down the vision and make it understandable is that you are going to encounter the inevitable—distractions. All the time you were wandering, distractions did not seem to bother you—at least not consciously. Now that you are on the right path to becoming great and changing the world, and everything is going to come at you at once. That is why having and knowing a clear direction is imperative. You must also understand that not every distraction is going to be bad. I would say the majority of the distractions you will face will be in the form of good opportunities. These opportunities are ones that would be good to participate in and do not seem harmful. However, participating in the "good" opportunities will get you off track and further delay you from your purpose. The most powerful word that should be in your vocabulary from now on, and which should be used often, is "No." Yes, that's right—*no*! This word scares a lot of people, especially those of us who have dealt with people-pleasing. We have to know it is okay to say no when something does not line up with where we are going. If one of those opportunities were meant to be, it would come back around at its proper time. You must have a streamlined focus because many people's lives are dependent on you birthing this vision God gave you.

I highly recommend you create a vision board to serve as a constant reminder where you are going. Call some friends over and make it a party. Making a vision board should be fun and exciting because you have reached a milestone many people do not get to in life. Put the vision board someplace, where you will see it every day. Take a picture of it and save it as your screensaver on your desktop and cell phone. You want to be reminded continuously throughout the day what you are working towards and where you are going.

GOALS

Remember earlier in this chapter when you read this quote:

> "A dream written down with a date becomes a goal. A goal broken down into steps becomes a plan. A plan backed by action makes your dreams come true."

Well, this is where you put this into action. God dreams are *huge*, and they take time to come to fruition. One thing is for sure—if you are not careful, the vision can become overwhelming if it is not broken down into bite-size pieces. Making goals requires much thought and planning, but the moment you have it written out in steps—with deadlines, then you are on your way to your dreams.

I love the book called "The One Thing" by Gary Keller because it teaches us about focusing on goal setting. It's not your average book because other professionals may say crush all your goals. However, Gary Keller says you should crush one goal at one time. He instructs the reader to ask themselves this question: "What's the ONE Thing I could do, such that by doing it, everything else would be easier or unnecessary?" [6]

That question makes you really focus on what goal is important. It should work like a domino effect. The first accomplished goal knocks down the next until it forms a ripple effect.

Start with the big-picture goal. Where do you see yourself in five years? Three years? One year? Once you get to the one-year goal, break that down into action steps on what you can do in the next month, next week, next day, and even to the next hour. Working backward provides you clarity on what needs to happen to reach those bigger goals.

ACCOUNTABILITY

Hear me clearly when I say this. *You will get discouraged along the journey.* I'm sorry if this sounds negative, but it's the truth. Anytime you make progress forward, there will be things that work against you—family issues that arise out of nowhere, unexpected incidents that occur. If you can name it, it will happen. Even when these things come along, you have to push through because your purpose is too important. That is why you need an accountability partner(s).

An accountability partner is someone who knows your goals and holds you accountable to ensure you stay on track. Get someone who won't take any excuses from you and who can motivate and encourage you along the way. Your accountability partner should also be someone who has seen results in their own life, somebody you look up to and admire. An unmotivated person cannot motivate you to reach your full potential when they are not doing so themselves.

When I was writing this book, I had an accountability partner who made me send him a chapter a week until I was finished with the book. He had already achieved what I was trying to accomplish because he was a published author. His story inspired me because he had someone do the same for him. Throughout the process, hard things came up in my life, and I stopped writing. My accountability partner stuck with me, checked in, motivated, and challenged me to keep going. Greatness has a price, and it requires discipline.

Discipline requires you to do things when you don't "feel" like it. The same will go for you. Go ahead and throw the "feelings" out of the window because you have to have a focused mentality that you must get this goal completed no matter what.

TEAM WORK MAKES THE DREAM WORK

I know the saying, "Teamwork makes the dream work." That is so true! You will not be able to pursue a Godly dream without help. Go ahead and start praying on who those people are to be on your team. Those people will always come as you progress in your vision. People are attracted to movement, and so is God. Faith moves God. Once you finish one step, go to the next. All of a sudden, you will meet someone that does or has what you need.

Your team will consist of many people with different skills and attributes. Every member should complement one another. No one should have the same skill set until the organization grows astronomically. Then you are going to need more people in the same area. Once your vision is written down, write down your ideal role and person to fit that role. What skills do they possess? What expertise is needed? For example, if a team's ratio is 5:1000, then when the organization doubles, each position should double. You'll need a marketing strategist and an assistant, a lead CPA, and an assistant CPA. Growth requires systems and efficiency.

EXECUTE WITH EXCELLENCE

One word that should be in your vocabulary, and that describes your work ethic, is excellence. That is correct. *Excellence.* When you are representing and pursuing a Godly dream, the result should be an excellent product, organization, system, etc. We can no longer settle. We were not created for mediocrity but greatness. When you are working, give it 110% the entire time. This verse always challenges me as I am working on different projects:

> Work willingly at <u>whatever</u> you do, as though you were working for the Lord rather than people. (Colossians 3:23)

Wow! That is a game-changer! It says work willingly at *whatever* you do. Everything you do should be done in excellence and nothing less. You have to ask yourself, *Is this final product excellent or thrown together? Did I serve my clients and constituents well, or did I do them a disservice?* These things matter when it comes to your purpose because you are an example. You are a world-changer, and world-changers are not sloppy or lazy. They are role models and great examples of how when your work is excellent you get to experience great things in this life.

Now the ball is in your court. It is up to you to take all the lessons learned from this book and apply them to your life. I emphasize "apply" because an action is required. Do not let this be just another book that you read and put it down never to pick back up again. I hope that my transparency about my struggles helps you to understand that you are not alone, and you can move forward in life. Pain is temporary. What you do with that pain is a different story. I highly suggest you turn that pain into an account to help others. Trust the process of your healing. It is a long and gruesome process, but it is so worth it. Your Godly dreams will come alive, and that will make an impact on this world. The world is waiting for you to walk in your true calling. Will you answer that call? Live now!

BIBLIOGRAPHY

1. "innocence." *Merriam-Webster.com*. 2019. https://
   www.merriam-webster.com/dictionary/innocence (24
   September 2019).

2. Whitbourne, Susan. (2012, August 11). "The
   Definitive Guide to Guilt." Retrieved September 24,
   2019, from https://www.psychologytoday.com/us/blog/
   fulfillment-any-age/201208/the-definitive-guide-guilt

3. Kirkpatrick, Nicola. (2018, December 14). "Guilt
   Vs. Shame: What's the Difference and Why
   Does It Matter?" Retrieved September 24, 2019,
   from https://www.betterhelp.com/advice/guilt/
   guilt-vs-shame-whats-the-difference-and-why-does-it-
   matter/

4. Vassar, Gerry. (2011, April 7). "Understanding
   Toxic Shame." Retrieved September 24, 2019,
   from https://lakesidelink.com/blog/lakeside/
   understanding-toxic-shame/.

5. Greg Reid Quote - https://www.goodreads.com/author/
   quotes/905034.Greg_Reid

6. Keller, Gary, and Jay Papasan. *The One
   Thing: The Surprisingly Simple Truth behind
   Extraordinary Results*. Bard Press, 2017.

ABOUT THE AUTHOR

ISIAH D. TATUM is a dreamer, visionary, and leader whose life's goal is to help others discover purpose in life. Each person is born with greatness inside but has a limited amount of time to achieve that greatness. He believes the only way to tap into greatness is to serve people, overcome fear, and create the life you've always dreamed of obtaining. Tatum vows to die empty and leave a legacy that will inspire generations to dream.

He is a serial entrepreneur in Real Estate, Film, TV, and Music, and owns Big I's Sweet Potato Pies. Isiah is a native of Little Rock, Arkansas, and he graduated from Arkansas State University and received a Master's in Entertainment Business from Full Sail University.

In 2015, Isiah authored and self-published *Finding That Business In You,* an e-book on entrepreneurship, which has impacted the lives of many people. Most notably, *Finding That Business in You* was adopted into the curriculum of the B.E.S.T. (Building Entrepreneurs for Success in Tennessee) Program in the Tennessee Department of Correction.

CPSIA information can be obtained
at www.ICGtesting.com
Printed in the USA
LVHW082044170220
647250LV00003B/5

9 781640 857209